LIVING WITH NO
Regrets

Harrison House

Shippensburg, PA

GET READY FOR YOUR FUTURE
BY GETTING OVER YOUR PAST

LIVING WITH NO
Regrets

GREG FRITZ

Living with No Regrets

13 digit ISBN 978-1-68031-214-0

Ebook 13 ISBN 978-1-68031-279-9

LP ISBN 978-1-68031-280-5

HC ISBN 978-1-68031-281-2

Copyright © 2019 by Greg Fritz

Published by Harrison House Publishers
P.O. Box 310
Shippensburg, Pennsylvania 17257-0310

www.harrisonhouse.com

Endorsements

To have your best life now, you have to get over the past mistakes in your life—we all have them. Greg has opened up the truth of God's Word, so that you can experience the "good life" and walk in victory with "no more regrets."

—Pastor Mike Davis
Rocky Mountain Family Church
Pueblo, Colorado

I heartily recommend this book. This message brings freedom and healing to those who receive it. I have known Greg Fritz for 30 years. He is an excellent teacher, and his life represents the gospel he proclaims!

—Pastor Lawson Perdue
Charis Christian Center
Colorado Springs, Colorado

There are books that are informative, and there are books that are transformative. *Living With No Regrets* was transformative to my life. It wiped away decades of "what ifs" that held sway over me. This revelation will break the chains of looking back. The wonderment of past missteps will no longer haunt your life. Let this book create a change in your life that will bring new freedom to your future.

—Senior Pastor Sam Carr

Contents

Foreword

Regret is a prison of our own making. It holds us captive to the past and prevents us from enjoying the present and looking forward to the future. Sadly, we sometimes lock the door and throw away the key to this prison, thinking there is no hope. But this book is bringing you good news. Jesus can pick any lock, break any chain, and overcome any demonic jailer that tries to keep you bound. You really can live with no regrets.

I admit this is easier said than done, but it can and must be done—and it has been done. In this book is a dramatic testimony from Carol Fritz, Greg's wife, who has overcome more guilt, condemnation, and regret than most of us will ever have to deal with. That one chapter is well worth the read.

But there is so much more. Greg deals with this topic from every angle. As one of the most popular guest speakers at our Charis Bible College and at my Gospel Truth Conferences, Greg has allowed the Lord to minister through him with supernatural results—I've seen it. This book will be no different. This book contains the key to setting you free.

Most of us have used a GPS device to navigate. If you are like me, you don't always follow the instructions perfectly and have missed a turn. But the GPS knows exactly where you are and instantly recalculates to get you from where you are back to where you are supposed to be. God is much greater than any man-made GPS system. If the route guide can get you back on course, how much more can the Lord put you back on track, regardless of how many bad turns you have made! You just have to receive.

Everyone's situation is unique, but there is only one answer. Jesus is more than enough for whatever life has thrown at you. I pray the Holy Spirit quickens the truths in this book to your heart and sets you free. Freedom and a life of no regrets is His will for you. Receive it!

—Andrew Wommack
President and Founder
Andrew Wommack Ministries, Inc.
Charis Bible College

Introduction

Living with no regrets isn't just the title of this book. It's a way of life. It can be a reality for every child of God. It can be a reality for *you!* No matter what you've been through, what you've done, or what's been done to you, you can be free from the experiences of the past and live life to the fullest with no regrets. This teaching is founded upon one simple truth: What Jesus has done is enough to set you free from your past.

Jesus paid the price for you through His redemptive work on the cross, and freedom is available *now.* Applying this powerful truth in a personal way to past experiences is the best way—sometimes the only way—to get free from regrets. You have so much to live for! But you cannot drive forward on the road of life while looking at the past in the rear-view mirror. Sorrow, sadness, guilt, and shame is not God's will for your life regardless of what you've done.

Revelation 21:4 says, "God will wipe away every tear from their eyes...." This scripture is talking about a day in the future when we're in heaven and God the Father will personally wipe away our tears. These tears represent regrets of all varieties—wrong choices, missed opportunities, failures, and heartbreaks. In heaven, God will completely remove the stains and scars left by sin and all the other negative experiences of life.

For years, I've enjoyed preaching on this verse and looking forward to this wonderful day when sin and evil will be no more, and we'll forever be free from the effects of the past. But we don't have to wait until we get to heaven to be free of regrets. We can have freedom now!

This revelation has changed my life. Freedom from anything that causes regret in this life has already been paid for on the cross. We can live free not because of what we've done but because of what He's done! God isn't going to do a new thing in heaven when He wipes away our tears. He will just fully apply a redemption that is *already ours.* We can apply the same truths today and enjoy freedom from the past right now.

Jesus paid such a high price for our failures, the last thing He wants us to do is spend our lives looking back with regret. It's time to move on! God has big plans for your future!

Let's get ready for the future by getting over the past. For most, this is a process. Yet, when the scriptures included in this book are properly applied over time, you will know the truth and the truth will make you free. God's Word works! Read on and find out how to get the whine out of your voice and live the life you were meant to live with joy inexpressible and full of glory!

No more sadness. No more sorrow. No more regrets.

CHAPTER 1

DESTROYING
Disappointment

Regret \ ri-'gret \

a feeling of sorrow or remorse for a fault, act, loss, disappointment

Living with regrets can be crippling. Sorrow and remorse over past experiences can rob you of joy and vision and hinder you from living the life God has for you. He wants to help you get over the past and get ready for God's best for your life. Some folks need to quit trying to figure out all the details concerning their past and their future. It's not right to be held hostage by painful past experiences and bad memories. Jesus has paid the price to set us free! He set us free to be happy, joyful, peaceful, and filled with anticipation.

When it comes to regret, we as Christians have a choice to make. It's as clear cut as life and death and blessing and cursing.

Deuteronomy 30:19

I call heaven and earth as witnesses today against you, that I have set before you life and death, blessing and cursing; therefore choose life, that both you and your descendants may live.

It is possible to live a life without regret, but the choice is up to you. Choose life! No matter how much you've done right, Satan wants you to choose to regret your past. No matter how much you've done wrong, Jesus can set you free from regrets. In fact, your experiences, good or bad, don't determine your state of mind, just like your possessions don't determine your level of happiness. I've been to some of the poorest nations on earth and met people who have next to nothing, yet they're happy. On the other hand, I've met people who have nearly everything money can buy, yet they're miserable. It's all about choices. One person chooses happiness

> It is possible to live a life without regret, but the choice is up to you. Choose life!

and the other chooses misery. Your life doesn't have to be the sum total of all your bad experiences, but if you focus on regrets, you're making a choice that leads to bitterness, sadness, and remorse.

The enemy wants you to spend your life looking back and rehearsing all the things you could have done differently. There will always be things you could have done but you did not do, or you should not have done but you did do that cannot be changed now. You know it's the enemy when you get all exercised about something that you couldn't change if you wanted to.

> You need to march into your future with no strings attached—nothing to hold you back, nothing to threaten or intimidate you, nothing to remind you of past failures.

What good does it do now to regret or to mourn things that cannot be changed? There's a point in time when you just have to move on and say, "I may not be perfect, but I'm still going to do the will of God with my life. God has a plan for me. He has an anointing for me. And I'm going to accomplish all He has for my future."

You need to march into your future with no strings attached—nothing to hold you back, nothing to threaten or intimidate you, nothing to remind you of past failures. Satan wants to take experiences from your past and use them to build a case against you. He wants to prove beyond a reasonable doubt that you'll never be able to do what God has told you to do or be what God has told you to be. That's a lie! With God on your side, your past actually can prepare you for the future no matter what happened.

Sadness, sorrow, mourning, and regret persist because of experiences that are part of your history. You can either get over them, or you can experience grief and sorrow for the rest of your life. I'd rather get over it. Maybe you've felt as if you need permission to get over the negative effects of your past. God's Word gives you that permission. We're going to look at scriptures that will enable you to leave the past behind and move into your future with no regrets.

Hebrews 12:1

*Therefore we also, since we are surrounded by so great a cloud of witnesses, **let us lay aside every weight, and the sin which so easily ensnares us.***

Some of these regrets we're talking about are sins and some are weights, but both need to go. They're history!

Unfortunately, nobody can remind you of your failures like your relatives. In fact, sometimes when folks get right with God and really start to make progress or get in Church or Bible school, relatives say, "Oh, don't you give me that act. I know *you*. I know what *you* did. I know who *you* are!" But the apostle Paul said, "I don't know anybody after the flesh" (2 Corinthians 5:16).

I don't know what you **were** in the flesh either, but I can tell you what you are in the spirit. If you're born again, you're a new creation and the righteousness of God. That means you're forgiven, you're blameless, you're an overcomer, and you have God living in you. Greater is He that is in you, than he that is in the world. You can do whatever God has called you to do. Your past cannot disqualify you from the future God has for you.

Really, the only reason for Christians to regret the past is because they haven't properly applied what Jesus did to what they did. Some will say, "Well, you don't know what I did." Well, maybe you don't know what Jesus did! I promise you that what He did will cancel out what you did. So, you can get over it!

Through the teaching in this book, I want to eradicate sorrow, mourning, sadness, and regret from your life! Whatever is causing these things, God's message to you is this: It's time to get over it, and get on with your life.

Revelation 21:4

And God will wipe away every tear from their eyes; there shall be no more death, nor sorrow, nor crying. There shall be no more pain, for the former things have passed away.

These tears represent regrets. They are the results of scars left from life on earth or the residue left on your being from living life in a fallen world. Yet, God doesn't want your past to ruin your eternity. God wants you living the abundant life—no more tears, no more sorrow, no more regret! If God wipes away your tears, there won't be anything left to cry about.

Jesus died for you, and the price has been paid! He removed sin, failure, guilt, condemnation. You can apply what Jesus did to your past and be free now! You don't have to wait until you get to heaven to live with no regrets and be happy.

When the Father comes to you in heaven and says, "I've come to wipe away your tears." You can say, "I already took care of that. I applied the blood of Jesus to my life, and it totally set me free. I've been laughing for years now. All is well!"

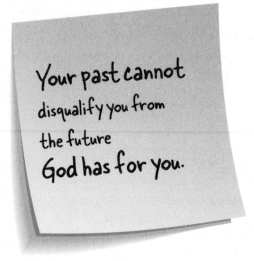

Your past cannot disqualify you from the future God has for you.

CHAPTER 2

GREAT JOY
to All People

When the angel appeared to the shepherds to announce the birth of Jesus in Luke 2:10, it says, "Then the angel said to them, 'Do not be afraid, for behold, I bring you good tidings of great joy which will be to all people.' Aren't you glad we live in the day of good tidings and great joy to all people? Yet, you cannot have great joy if you're in mourning over your past. You cannot have great joy if you can't get over what you've done or what somebody did to you. You cannot have great joy if you can't seem to get through some experience that you had earlier in life. So, leave the past in the past where it belongs. It's time to have great joy! It's for *all people* to have great joy, and that includes you!

We have a good message. We have good tidings. We have good news. We have something good to share that creates joy in the listener. This is not mind over matter, and we aren't trying to cope by saying, "I'm just going to ignore my past." No, your past has already been dealt with legally. Jesus said, "The Spirit of the Lord is upon me. He has anointed Me to preach the gospel to the poor and heal the brokenhearted."

Maybe you've endured tragedy or crisis or loss in your life, and your heart is broken. There's no psychiatrist in the world who can heal a broken heart. There's no surgeon in the world who can operate on a broken heart. And there's no drug that can heal a broken heart. But Jesus can do something about it! He can heal your broken heart. The Holy Spirit working through God's Word can heal and remove sorrow, grief, mourning, and pain and make you better than you were before. It has worked for others, and it can work for you. So, prepare to be healed.

I was reading a book by a minister who was teaching about prayer, and he mentioned praying for someone who had a need. After they had agreed in prayer and the person left, the minister said, "I knew the person didn't receive his answer because after we had agreed in prayer, he still had a whine in his voice." I was convicted when I read that! I realized I was guilty of having a whine in my voice concerning some of the experiences of the past. I began to see how subtle sorrow, sadness, and regret can be. They can enter your thoughts and remain lodged in your mind because of real experiences you seemingly cannot forget.

Even if regrets don't overwhelm you, a subtle little nag can drain your energy like an app running in the background draining the battery on a cell phone. You might have been like me and not really noticed that you were being robbed of joy and happiness. You might not have realized that every time you thought or talked about certain experiences, your words were filled with sadness, sorrow, and regret.

We all have reasons we harbor regrets, but let's make sure we have no whine in our voices. Let's believe God and take Him at His Word.

First Peter 1:8 says:

Whom having not seen you love, [that is Jesus.] *Though now you do not see Him, yet believing, you rejoice with joy inexpressible and full of glory.*

Choose not to settle for anything less than joy unspeakable and full of glory. You can have joy manifested in your life that's so great and so consuming it cannot be described. You won't be able to tell people why you're so happy.

How will that happen? It will happen because "yet believing, you rejoice" in Him. It's not because you look back and don't have anything to be sorry about. Let's face it, if you live long enough, you'll have plenty to be sorry about. But we're filled with joy because of what He did, not because of what we did! I don't see the word *sorrow* in 1 Peter 1:8. What I do see is that if you will believe in Him, you can rejoice with joy unspeakable and full of glory.

Romans 8:11 (KJV)

But if the Spirit of him that raised up Jesus from the dead dwell in you, he that raised up Christ from the dead shall also quicken your mortal bodies by his Spirit that dwelleth in you.

It will make a difference in your life if you go around saying to yourself, "The same spirit that raised Christ from the dead dwells in me. The Spirit of God dwells in my body." Sadness, sorrow, regrets, and a whole lot of other things that should never hang onto Christians will drop off.

John G. Lake lived over a hundred years ago and was powerfully used of God to preach the gospel and heal the sick. He wrote that every morning when he woke up he would look in the mirror and say to himself out loud, "God lives in that man." If you're a Christian, that is also true about you. And it will make a huge difference in your life when you begin to realize it.

Romans 8:11 helped set me free from regret more than any other scripture. Say it continually and meditate on the fact that the same spirit that raised Christ from the dead "lives in me." Think about it. The

Choose not to settle for anything less than joy unspeakable and full of glory.

24

same power that defeated death and Satan and all principalities and powers, lives in you. *You* have GOD living in *you*. Every time I speak that scripture, life flows into me, and my mind is renewed. My thoughts change. Joy and peace displace grief and sorrow.

> God is big enough to make up for your past if you'll let Him.

Have you ever gotten into the presence of God and found Him to be depressed, sad, or sorrowful? No. God is never depressed, and He changes not. He's totally unaffected by earthly events. So, if He's not sad, then I'm not going to be sad. If He's not living in grief and regret, then I'm not going to either. He's the same yesterday, today, and forever (Hebrews 13:8). He paid the price, so we can be as free as He is. We can react to life on earth as He does. The Word of God says as He is so are we in this world (1 John 4:17).

God isn't nervous. He isn't wringing His hands, looking back at the past wondering what could have been. He doesn't wonder, *What if? What if this hadn't happened? What if that had of happened? What if I hadn't made that decision?* No, God doesn't think that way, and you shouldn't either. The truth is, God is big enough to make up for your past if you'll let Him. He is the God of the second chance, the third chance, the fourth chance, and as many chances as you need. God can still work in your life. He'll give you yet another chance. The question is, will you give Him one? Will you give yourself one? Many people disqualify themselves. But God still has a plan for you.

You might be saying, "You don't know what I've done." No, but God does. And He can still use you. There's much work to be done. God needs people who aren't bound by the past, aren't held back with regret, and aren't sad or sorrowful. These things affect your faith and limit your ability to serve God.

Let's look at Ephesians 1:3-7:

> *...who has **blessed** us with every spiritual blessing in the heavenly places in Christ, just as He **chose** us in Him before the foundation of the world, that we should be **holy** and **without blame** before Him in love, having predestined us to **adoption** as sons by Jesus Christ to Himself, according to the good pleasure of His will, to the praise of the glory of His grace, by which He made us **accepted** in the Beloved. In Him we have **redemption** through His blood, the **forgiveness** of sins, according to the riches of His grace.*

Now, apply these verses to your situation. You're blessed, chosen, holy, blameless, adopted, accepted, redeemed, and forgiven. God wants you to be in His family and live life together with you. Whatever you've done, whatever you've been through, and whatever baggage you've been carrying because of your past is no match for what Jesus has done to set you free.

God hasn't changed His mind about you. Romans 11:29 says, "God does not change his mind about whom he chooses and blesses" (GNT). So, get up, and get ready to move on with God. You can do anything God has promised you can do. Give Him another chance to fulfill His promises in your life.

2 Corinthians 5:21

He made Him who knew no sin to be sin for us. That we might be made the righteousness of God in Him.

Jesus took your sin and all its consequences, so you could be made the righteousness of God. God's ability to complete His plan in your life is not possible because of what *you did* but because of what *He did*. We ought to be the happiest people on earth because we can exchange sadness and sorrow for gladness and joy.

Let's look at an Old Testament promise that has New Testament application.

Psalm 126:1-3

When the Lord brought back the captivity of Zion, we were like those who dream. Then

*our mouth was **filled with laughter, and our
tongue with singing**. Then they said among
the nations, "The LORD has done great things
for them." **The LORD** has done great things
for us, **and** we are glad.*

In this scripture, Zion is a type or example of the New Testament Church. In other words, it represents you and me. It represents when the Lord redeemed us, and it should be our confession today! Our mouths should be filled with laughter and singing as we rejoice saying, "The Lord has done great things for us and we are glad!" Notice it does not say anything about being sorry or sad. No, it says we have a right to be glad, and we ought to be. Jesus paid a high price for us to be glad.

The last chapter of this book includes many scriptures, which you can read aloud and say over and over to counteract the negative effects of regret in your life. You may want to skip ahead to chapter 13 and speak these words of life daily while you read through this book. Say them over and over again until you drive out every bit of sadness and sorrow, every bit of regret in your life. This is the beginning of a powerful transformation in your life. May God's Spirit flood you with light as you get ready for your future by getting over your past.

CHAPTER 3

HE RESTORES
My Soul

One of the blessings that comes from the hand of the good Shepherd in the 23rd Psalm is that He restores the soul.

> *He makes me to lie down in green pastures;*
> *He leads me beside the still waters.* ***He***
> ***restores my soul;*** *He leads me in the paths of*
> *righteousness For His name's sake.*

Many Christians are quick to apply God's Word to their spirits when they become born again and forgiven of sin. Some stand boldly on God's Word for healing in their bodies, which is also one of the many benefits of being in the Lord's sheepfold. But there is another benefit that is often overlooked in the area of the soul. We are three-part beings. We are a spirit, we have a soul, and we live in a body

(1 Thessalonians 5:23). Jesus paid the price to redeem all three parts of man.

The soul is made up of the mind, will, and emotions. It is easy to see how events from the past can leave their mark on the mind and emotions. This is where feelings of sadness, sorrow, guilt, and regret reside. Some people look fine on the outside, but they are literally handicapped in their minds because of past experiences. God's Word and His delivering power can be applied to the soul as well as to the spirit and body. Jesus paid the price to undo all that sin has done to the soul. Hence, God's Word says, "He restores my soul."

Life has a way of doing damage to the body and the soul. Yet, no matter how much damage has been done, Jesus has done more than enough to restore it. It isn't necessary to have a degree in psychology to help people in this area. I don't have to be a medical doctor to offer God's healing power to someone's body, and I don't have to be a psychiatrist to offer God's healing power to restore a soul. The gospel we preach has within it the power to heal the brokenhearted, deliver the captives, and set at liberty those who are oppressed and downtrodden (Luke 4:18). Part of our job description as New Testament ministers is to minister restoration to the soul.

> It may be true that you'll never be the same after what you've been through, but with God you can be better than before.

God's power through His Word can do amazing miracles in this area.

Psalm 30:11-12

You have turned for me my mourning into dancing; You have put off my sackcloth and clothed me with gladness, to the end that my glory may sing praise to You and not be silent. O Lord my God, I will give thanks to You forever.

What medical professional would even pretend to do this for someone suffering from long-term grief and mourning? Most people would be happy to go from mourning to some semblance of normal. Yet, God's Word promises to take the mourner so far from mourning, they won't be able to find their way back. It may be true that you'll never be the same after what you've been through, but with God you can be better than before. Only God can turn your mourning into dancing. He's able to replace sadness with gladness in your life, so you can be happy again!

We see redemption for the whole man in Isaiah 53:5:

But He was wounded for our transgressions, He was bruised for our iniquities **[spirit]***; The chastisement for our peace was upon Him* **[soul]***, And by His stripes we are healed* **[body]***.*

The chastisement for our peace, or the punishment necessary for us to have peace, was put upon Jesus. Just as divine healing is for the physical body, divine peace is for the soul. If your mind is dominated by thoughts of sorrow and regret and your emotions are flooded with feelings of sadness, guilt, and condemnation, you aren't experiencing divine peace. But it belongs to you! Some Christians have never realized that they don't have to be dominated by thoughts and feelings of regret no matter what they've done.

In fact, freedom from regret is just as much part of our redemption as forgiveness of sin and healing for the body. Because of this lack of understanding, many allow themselves to be held hostage by past events and never really apply the Word of God to this area of their lives. I know there are lots people who need this teaching. I have many CD series available on my website and always offer them in my meetings, but the audio series *Living with No Regrets* has outsold any other series in my library. It's time to get this message out! It's time for you to get over the past and be happy again!

> Freedom from regret is just as much part of our redemption as forgiveness of sin and healing for the body.

FIGHT FOR PEACE

If someone were to come through your front door and announce they were going to rob your house, you would probably fight them tooth and nail. However, some folks let the devil come in every day and rob them of joy, happiness, and peace. They allow him to convince them that because of past experiences they should be sad or depressed. They believe that because of what's happened in their past they should never be happy again, or they will never be what they could have been. Don't believe those lies!

Satan cannot huff and puff and blow your house down like the big bad wolf. He cannot overcome you by brute force, so he gains entrance through lies and deception. He will try to convince you to let him in voluntarily. He will use facts you are very familiar with to make the case that you should be sad or depressed or miserable. Thoughts will come saying, *After all, look what you've done. Look what you've been through. Look what they did to you. Look what they didn't do for you.* That's why the Word tells you to give no place to the devil (Ephesians 4:27). That means if the devil has a place, you gave it to him. Even if you did give it to him, take it back!

A wave of negative emotions will flood your soul if you agree with the lies that bombard your mind. Refuse to allow those thoughts into your mind as if you're resisting a thief at the front door of your house. Some people are bold and outspoken in other areas, but when it comes to guarding their minds from thoughts of failure, guilt, sadness and shame, they are wimpy. They allow the enemy to bully them into a

Refuse to allow those thoughts into your mind as if you're resisting a thief at the front door of your house.

state of depression without even putting up a fight.

An example of this is the feeling of loneliness. You can be alone without being lonely. Yet many times, the enemy uses these situations and circumstances to get folks to accept something that doesn't belong to them. Thoughts come such as, *You're alone. You've never been alone before. You've always had other family members in your home, and now you're the only one left. Everybody has somebody but you. You should be sooo lonely.* No! Resist that thought! Fight against it. Don't let the enemy steal your peace. You may be alone, but you don't have to be lonely. You may have failed, but you're not a failure. You may have sinned, but you're not a sinner. You may have missed opportunities in your life, but you don't have to live with regret. Don't let the enemy come in and set up shop in your soul.

John 14:27

Peace I leave with you, My peace I give to you; not as the world gives do I give to you. Let not your heart be troubled, neither let it be afraid.

The peace that Jesus has provided is not like the world's peace. The world has peace when everything is peaceful, but the peace of God is a force that can keep your soul even in difficult times. God's peace is independent of circumstances. You can have peace despite what's happened because of what Jesus has done for you. You may have abuse, tragedy, and failure in your past, but the peace that Jesus gives is not dependent on what happened to you. It's yours because of what happened to Him. The chastisement of our peace was upon Him.

Jesus said, "Let not your heart be troubled, neither let it be afraid." Don't exchange your peace for fear or sadness or sorrow. Fight for what is yours! Quit allowing Satan to bully you with lies and defeat him with the truth. Get tough in your mind! Don't be carried away with any and every thought that comes your way. Exercise discipline in your thought life, or you'll live life on an emotional roller coaster where you're up one day and down the next. Or worse, you'll be down one day and further down the next.

2 Corinthians 10:4-5 (KJV)

For the weapons of our warfare are not carnal, but mighty through God to the pulling down of strong holds; Casting down imaginations, and every high thing that exalteth itself against the knowledge of God, and bringing into captivity every thought to the obedience of Christ.

Take every thought captive! Control what comes into your mind and screen your thoughts with the Scriptures.

There are Christians who live life with a cloud of depression hanging over their heads every day. They would never allow sin in their life or sickness to enter their bodies, but they give place to depression every single day. They have believed a lie, such as, "After all you've been through, you ought to be depressed." They should believe the truth, which is, "After all Jesus has done, I could never be depressed!" We should be the happiest people on earth! Why? Because the Bible is true. God is still on the throne. Jesus is Lord. And we're going to heaven!

You can be proactive instead of reactive in prayer and allow peace to dominate your heart and your mind.

Philippians 4:6-7

Be anxious for nothing, but in everything by prayer and supplication, with thanksgiving, let your requests be made known to God; and the peace of God, which surpasses all understanding, will guard your hearts and minds through Christ Jesus.

Notice how the fruit of peace can guard your heart and mind when it's released through prayer. When something in your life is especially troubling and producing feelings of sadness and sorrow every time you think about it, pray about it. Then, let Jesus make up the difference for your faults and failures and give you peace in return. A heart and mind that's guarded by peace is not full of sorrow and sadness, worry, and fear.

As you begin to agree with God and speak His Word in these areas, good thoughts and feelings will follow.

2 Timothy 1:7

For God has not given us a spirit of fear, but of power and of love and of a sound mind.

Anything less than a sound (in good condition, not damaged, not injured) mind is not the will of God. Apply God's Word to your soul by speaking and meditating on it. I have included many scriptures and confessions in the last chapter, which have helped me tremendously along these lines. It would be helpful—even life changing—if you will turn there now and begin to speak these promises over your life. If you begin now and continue while reading this book, the information we cover in the upcoming chapters will have a much greater impact upon your life.

CHAPTER 4

MISSED
Opportunities

Everyone can look back over their past and create a list of missed opportunities. They think, *I could have done this. I should have done that.* Thoughts of "would've, could've, should've" can hound us all. Yet, now that we've established that living with no regrets is the will of God, it's important to examine some of these instances in life that cause regret. It helps us stop the past from threatening our future.

For example, some people who are now in their 50s and 60s may regret the fact they didn't have kids when they could have. Others may regret they did! Or some may regret missing investment opportunities that are no longer possible. I wish I had purchased Apple stock when it was cheap. I could have but I didn't, and it's not cheap anymore. I could have gotten rich off the stock market. I should have purchased

Wal-Mart stock 30 years ago, but I didn't. How long must we spend looking back with regret? We have a future, and it's not in the past.

Some people use the past to escape responsibility for the future. "I should have tried out for the NFL." "I was a good player. My life would have been different if I had only taken a chance." What good does that do now that you're 40 years old and overweight? That train has left the station! You probably wouldn't have made the team anyway! Too much of this kind of reflection can become an excuse to hide behind, and it prevents you from striving for excellence in the present.

In most cases like these, it's too late to go back and change things now, but the enemy wants to use these things to keep our attention focused on the past. It's much more difficult—even impossible—to go forward while looking backward. You have to say goodbye to certain things in the past, so you can be fully free to embrace the present and the future.

> You have to say goodbye to certain things in the past, so you can be fully free to embrace the present and the future.

Saying goodbye to the past is how you live big—live without limits—and believe God!

What good does it do to sit around and dream about what might have been? That's a waste of time. You may have heard this saying, "You can be anything you want to be."

That's an American saying, but I don't believe it's scriptural. I've seen too many people try to be something they're not. If you're 40 years old and overweight, you can't be an Olympic gymnast. I don't care how much you want it. But you can be anything God wants you to be. That's still possible. The truth is, the fulfillment of the promise is in the future, not the past. It's time to move on.

God knew you wouldn't do everything right. He's not angry and frustrated over your past, and you shouldn't be either. He's already made up for your mistakes, and He understands you and what you've been through.

Psalm 103:13-14 says, "As a father pities his children, so the Lord pities those who fear Him. He knows our frame, and he remembers that we are dust." God is well acquainted with the limitations we face as humans, and He's very sympathetic to our cause. He came and accomplished what was necessary, so we could be free from our past. Jesus paid the price of redemption, so we could be free from the mistakes, the sins of omission, and the sins of commission we are all too familiar with.

You are not unique in that sense—everybody has missed opportunities in life. God has done all that's necessary to allow you to

He's not angry and frustrated over your past, and you shouldn't be either.

forget the past and look forward to your future. Stop kicking yourself!

Over the years, we always tell new people who come to work for our ministry, "There are a hundred things to learn. You will make mistakes." Some of them think, *That was the last person, not me. I don't make mistakes.* Sure enough, eventually they do something wrong that costs time and money. But the problem isn't that a mistake was made; we expected that. We've found many times the problem is that some people have trouble going forward after the mistake because they're too hard on themselves.

Some people seem shocked that they actually did something wrong, and they grieve over it. They go on and on, beating themselves up because their performance wasn't perfect. We knew they weren't going to be perfect; nobody is. We knew something would happen sooner or later, and we're willing to pay for it. But we can't go forward and get back to work until they get over it.

God does the same thing! He knows our frame, and He's touched with the feeling of our infirmities (weaknesses, human limitations) (Hebrews 4:15). He knew we were going to make mistakes. He knew we weren't going to be perfect. He already paid for our mistakes, and He's ready for every one of us to move forward.

If this describes you, get over whatever it is holding you back! Apparently, you're the only one who's surprised; everyone else knew you weren't perfect! Don't take yourself too seriously. Quit looking back at all your shortcomings and stressing about what could've been if you had done things differently. You can't relive your past; you only have your future to live. Sometimes the only thing you can do about your past is get over it. God can do more with your future than you can do with your past.

Joel 2:25

So I will restore to you the years that the swarming locust has eaten, The crawling locust, The consuming locust, And the chewing locust....

God can restore years back to you that the swarming locust, the crawling locust, the consuming locust, and the chewing locust have eaten. In other words, God can restore back to you all that you lost because of bad choices, bad investments, and mistakes that cost you time and money. Through all the missed opportunities, God can still restore the years.

God knew what He was getting when He saved you and made promises to you. He built in the fact that you would mess up things, and He would make up the difference. Quit believing that because of your past you are

God can do more with your future than you can do with your past.

forever disqualified to live a happy and fruitful life in the will of God. He can redeem and restore and rebuild. The question is not: "How can I go back?" The question is: "Are you ready to go forward?"

If you will give God a chance, He can make more of your future than you could if you went back and lived the past again. You may have heard it said, He is the God of the second chances. The problem is not that God won't grant a second chance, but that people won't give Him a second chance. They are too willing to disqualify themselves because of what they have done or what they could have, would have, should have done.

Get out of the past and get on with your future. God doesn't have any "has-beens." God is the great *I Am*. And if God says, *I Am*, then you can be *I am* too! You don't need to be "I used to be" or "I almost was" or "I wish I was." In Him you are, and you can. Keep your attention on the present tense and the future tense because you can't go forward when you're looking back.

> Only Jesus made straight As in all the tests of life.

Many times, as you transition from one season to another you go through a time of reflection. When you graduate high school or college, you move away from home for the first time, you leave single life to get married, or you change jobs, the tendency is to reflect on the past. You look back with 20/20 vision, and then suddenly you realize what you could have done differently. It's easy to be critical and filled with regret as you realize how much better you could do if you could just do it over.

Many years ago, I was going through a transition like this as I moved into another area of ministry. As I looked back, I began to apologize to the Lord. I could see so many areas where I didn't do as well as I could have; I failed to do all that I could have done. I was sure if I could have gone back and done it over, I could have done so much better. Instead of joy over the future, I was experiencing grief and regret over the past. It was affecting my prayer life.

Finally, the Lord gave me an illustration. He showed me the previous season of my life represented as a type of college. He showed me that the different areas in my life that I was evaluating were like different courses or classes in college. He shared with me that in some courses I did very well and others not so well. Some areas I breezed through with ease while others were a struggle. He showed me that I wasn't a straight A student, and nobody is. Only Jesus made straight As in all the tests of life.

He concluded by saying, "You may not have scored well in every area, every course, or every relationship, but you passed. Today you're getting your diploma. You should have no more resentment or regret toward anyone or anything in this season of your life than you would have against a college professor who taught a difficult course you ultimately passed. You got what you came for—so no hard feelings, no regrets. You have your diploma, and it's time to move on!"

This truth has spoken to me time and time again over the years. We have freedom from the past. If you're still standing, if you still believe the Bible, and you still love the Lord, then you've passed some courses. You're still in the game, and God has a plan for you to fulfill. Quit focusing on the negatives and the failures of your past. You have your diploma from that season of life, and it's time to move on!

Nearly every doctor you visit has a diploma proudly displayed on their office wall. This serves as proof the doctor completed their education and earned the right to practice medicine. The diploma was earned by them performing at or above the minimum required standard set by the medical field. I've never seen a doctor post grade transcripts on the office wall because they probably don't want people to see all their grades. Hardly anyone makes straight As in medical school; that level of perfection is not necessary to become a doctor.

The diploma doesn't prove they are perfect, but it does prove they have learned enough to be your doctor. It would be fun to see their transcripts and question them about some of their lower grades. But in a practical sense, what good would it do for a doctor with a legitimate diploma from a reputable medical school to obsess over past scores? The diploma is proof that the time has come to move on! I don't want my doctor looking back, I want them focused on me here and now.

Oral Roberts was asked one time, "Have you ever made any mistakes in your ministry?" His reply was encouraging.

He said, "No, but I have discovered many ways to do things that don't work." He refused to allow the past to hold him hostage, and you should too. I'm so glad Oral Roberts didn't quit because he wasn't perfect. You may have done things that didn't work, but that doesn't mean you're a failure. Nobody but Jesus has aced the test of life!

Maybe you think you were the only one who missed opportunities in your past. Maybe you blame yourself and think things would be so different if you had taken advantage of these missed opportunities. You may think you could have really done something with your life had it been lived differently. You still can live differently! God can restore the years that have been stolen or wasted. He can still do what He promised to do for you. Give Him a second chance and believe that the best is yet to come.

Let's look at a few verses in this Psalm once again that change the focus from what you have done to what Jesus has done. Apply these verses to your life and situation:

Psalm 126:1-3

When the Lord brought back the captivity of Zion, we were like those who dream. Then our mouth was filled with laughter, and our tongue with singing. Then they said among the nations, "The Lord has done great things for them." The Lord has done great things for us, and we are glad.

Believe that God is able to do what He said. He can bring back your captivity and undo the effects of the past. It's time for you to let go of regret and get happy!

CHAPTER 5

PAST SINS

It's a shame for any Christian to suffer with guilt and condemnation after the high price Jesus paid to remove it. Yet, if not properly dealt with, the memory of past sins can cause plenty of problems. One of the reasons people have ongoing feelings of guilt and condemnation is because they're too focused on what they have done in the past. For forgiveness to be real, you must consider Jesus and what He did.

We're free because of what Jesus did. We can be glad because of what Jesus did. We can have happiness and joy unspeakable and full of glory because of what Jesus did. We can say goodbye forever to sadness, regret, mourning, and shame because of what Jesus did.

This is not a case of mind over matter. The answer is not to try harder to forget what you've done. If the Word is properly applied, old feelings of guilt and shame will give way to a sense of peace and assurance in Him.

Isaiah 53:5

He was wounded for our transgressions, He was bruised for our iniquities....

If the Word is properly applied, old feelings of guilt and shame will give way to a sense of peace and assurance in Him.

I don't totally understand how heaven's accounting system works. Yet taking God at His Word, it's clear that Jesus' suffering paid the penalty for your sins. Somehow, God used His death, suffering, and sacrifice to pay your debts. When Jesus was raised from the dead, your debt was canceled. Jesus solved the sin problem.

Forgiveness is real. It's available now, and it's yours. Some people believe Jesus can forgive them of small sins but not big ones. They harbor feelings of sadness and regret over some of the "big" sins in their past. Yet, Jesus either forgave us for all sins or He didn't forgive us for any sins. It's all or nothing. The truth is, Jesus' redemption works on **all** sin—big sin, little sin, old sin, new sin.

In fact, forgiveness is not just for sins you committed before you got saved. God didn't just wipe the slate clean when you got saved so you can fill it back up now that you're a Christian. Forgiveness isn't only for sinners. If it doesn't work for Christians also, then everyone's in trouble.

Somebody might say, "Yes, but I've done things since I got saved that I knew were wrong. I knew better and did it anyway." That's the very definition of sin.

"Yes, but other people were affected by my mistakes." That's what sin does.

"Yes, but I knew I shouldn't have." So did Adam.

We've all sinned and fallen short of the glory of God. That's why Jesus had to come. No one would make it without Him.

Matthew 1:21

*And she will bring forth a Son, and you shall call His name Jesus, for **He will save His people from their sins.***

We needed a Savior to save us from our sins. We were in over our heads, and we had no way out until He came.

Acts 5:31

Him [Jesus] *God has exalted to His right hand to be Prince and Savior, to give repentance to Israel and forgiveness of sins.*

It's crucial you understand the doctrine of forgiveness and apply it to your life. It's your ticket to freedom!

ONCE WAS ENOUGH

Hebrews 9:12

*Not with the blood of goats and calves, but with His own blood He entered the Most Holy Place **once for all**, having obtained eternal redemption.*

Hebrews 9:26

***Once at the end of the ages**, He has appeared to put away sin by the sacrifice of Himself.*

Hebrews 9:12 says "once for all," and Hebrews 9:26 above says "once at the end of the ages." How did Jesus do it? By the sacrifice of Himself. Did it work? Yes! That's why He only came once and only died once. In fact, the word *once* is vital to understanding forgiveness.

Hebrews 9:27-28

*And as it is appointed for men to die **once**, but after this the judgment, so Christ was offered **once** to bear the sins of many....*

Hebrews 10:10

By that [law] *will we have been sanctified through the offering of the body of Jesus Christ **once** for all.*

Again, the scripture says "once for all." The fact the Scriptures say *once* at least five times here in just a few verses proves it worked, because Jesus didn't have to try again. Jesus came once and returned to heaven not as a failure but as a success. Once was enough, He didn't have to do it twice. He didn't have to do it three times. He didn't have to do it four times. Jesus came once to deal with sins and wiped them out in our behalf.

Now let's add the word *all*. Hebrews 10:10 says "once for all."

That's where you come in. You are included in the "all." *All* means you and me and everybody else. There's no one that it didn't work for. You say, "You don't know what I've done." Aren't you something? So, you're the one person in all of history who did something so bad that Jesus' blood wasn't enough to pay for it? Is that what you believe? When you hold on to guilt, that's what you're saying. When you hold on to shame over past experiences, you're saying Jesus' death worked for everyone in the world but you. No, friend, that's a lie. Jesus died "once for all." *All* means *all* and all means *you!*

Hebrews 10:12

But this Man, after He had offered one sacrifice for sins forever, sat down at the right hand of God.

Jesus' mission was to purchase forgiveness for everyone. He was born, He died, He was buried, He was raised from the dead, He ascended to heaven, and He sat down. He sat down because He was finished. Mission accomplished. Jesus' one sacrifice was enough to provide forgiveness for everyone for all time. Jesus died one time. Jesus shed His blood one time. Jesus blood paid the debt completely and washed away all our sins one time because once was enough!

If Jesus is alive, the sin debt has been paid. Jesus' resurrection and our forgiveness of sins are linked together. There wouldn't be one without the other.

Romans 4:25

Who [Jesus] was delivered up because of our offenses, and was raised because of our justification.

If He's still dead, we are still in our sins, however, if He's alive, we're forgiven. Forgiveness is as real as the resurrection of Jesus!

1 Corinthians 15:17

And if Christ is not risen, your faith is futile; you are still in your sins!

But thank God, Jesus is alive! Our faith is profitable, and we are forgiven of our sins.

NO MORE MEMORY

Hebrews 10:17

Their sins and their lawless deeds I will remember no more.

If God says He will no longer remember your sins, you shouldn't remember them either. Many well-meaning Christian people ruin their prayer lives by getting in the presence

If God says He will no longer remember your sins, you shouldn't remember them either.

of God and constantly rehearsing their mistakes. God doesn't even know what they're talking about. He has forgiven and forgotten all their mistakes. Those sins are not being counted against them.

Think about this. If God said, "Their sins and lawless deeds I will remember no more," then why would you want to remember them? Quit ruining your prayer life by remembering things no longer on record. He wiped them out. Accept it!

Psalm 103:12

As far as the east is from the west, so far has He removed our transgressions from us.

People are very familiar with what they've done. They know it frontward, backward, and inside out. If they are repeat offenders, that adds to the compounded feelings of guilt and condemnation. I'm in no way trying to belittle sin. Quite the contrary, sin is awful. You should not have sinned, and the consequence should be hell forever. You should never be able to enter the presence of God again.

But God!

God made a way, and Jesus **is** that way.

You're once again welcome in the presence of God and free from whatever you've done in your past.

But to really get free from the past and move on, we need to talk about what Jesus did. He gave His life for our sins. He shed His blood, and He offered it as the eternal payment for the sins of the world. There is more value in one drop of that holy, spotless blood than anyone could ever imagine.

You may think, *But you don't know what I've done.* That's true. I don't know what you've done. You may have done a terrible wrong, and there may be a mountain of guilt in your past because of all you've done wrong. But that does not change the fact that the blood of Jesus was enough. It washed away your wrong and your guilt. The sacrifice Jesus made and offered to the Father is priceless and invaluable. He gave it once for all people—including you—forever. Accept what He did and apply it to your life. Believe the scripture in Hebrews that says, "Your sins and your lawless deeds I will remember no more."

Years ago, the cost of my car insurance got a little high, so I set out shopping for a new policy. That was some 20 years ago when I had been traveling in the ministry for only a few years. Back in those days, I drove to a lot of my meetings, and the more you drive, the more opportunities you have to get ticketed. The route to my meetings often took me through small towns. If I had a driving weakness, it was driving too fast through those small towns where the speed limit drops from 65 to 45. More than a few times, I had failed to pay close attention, and it cost me. I had a pretty nice collection of tickets from four or five different states.

Each time I called a new insurance company, they asked the same question, "Do you have any traffic tickets?"

"Yes! How many do you want?" I answered.

When I admitted that I had speeding tickets, they refused to check my history or even consider insuring me. The insurance company explained they go by the recorded history of your home state, and a person with traffic tickets on their record is not a good risk. They said I would have to wait three years for the tickets to fall off my record.

When there was no one else to call, I decided to go down to the Oklahoma Department of Motor Vehicles (ODMV) and see exactly how many tickets I had and how long I would have to wait. For $5.00, they did a search of my driving record. I was shocked when the results came back. They informed me that there were no tickets on my record and no points against me. I knew I had tickets from Nebraska, Kansas, Colorado, and Texas, but evidently, they didn't report them to Oklahoma. My record was clean!

I called the insurance company back. This time when they asked if I had any tickets, I told them to check my Oklahoma driving record. I said, "I have no tickets on my record and no points against me. You can check my records yourself for $5.00. I just checked. My record is clear." And I got the insurance for a discounted rate.

The insurance company wouldn't have taken my word for it anyway, whether I said I had tickets or not. They were going to verify it with the State of Oklahoma anyway. When they did, they found what I found, no tickets. If Oklahoma is okay with my record, and the insurance company is okay with my record, then I'm okay with my record. As far as the law was concerned, I was a perfect driver.

Look what Colossians 2:14 says about your record in the *Plain English Bible:*

> *He destroyed the record of the debts standing against us...He nailed it to the cross and put it out of sight.*

There are no records against you! Why take the time to remind God of something He's already forgotten? There is no record that you did anything wrong. Let it go.

The Inspired Letters in Clearest English by Frank Laubach translates Colossians 2:14 this way:

> *God crossed out the whole debt against us in His account books. He no longer counted the laws we had broken. He nailed the account book to the cross and closed the account.*

Case closed. God closed your account, and now you need to stand your ground and say, "The record against me is clean. The Judge has already ruled in my favor. I am acquitted. I am not guilty. I am sinless. God says I'm not guilty, and if God says I'm not guilty, then I will call myself not guilty."

You cannot add anything to what God has already done.

Hebrews 10:18

Where there is remission of these, there is no longer an offering for sin.

Don't try to pay for a debt that Jesus already paid. You cannot pay for it with tears. You cannot pay for it with grief. You cannot pay for it with sorrow. There's not a certain length of time that you need to mourn your past mistakes **because Jesus already paid for them.** All the tears that you could ever offer wouldn't pay for your sin. None of your blood would pay for your sin, and none of your repenting could ever pay for your sin. That's why you need to accept what Jesus did and move on. God has chosen to forgive you for all your sins forever. Now, your response is to say, "Thank you."

The fact that you're sorry and you grieve over your mistakes doesn't add to the price Jesus already paid. You can go forward with confidence as a forgiven, cleansed, purified, sanctified child of God. A lot of time is wasted by people who are trying to add to the price He paid, but it cannot be done. Accept forgiveness and move on!

CHAPTER 6

A GOD OF
Second Chances

Maybe you've thought you are disqualified from God's perfect will because of what you've done. Maybe you've felt as if God had great plans for you but after all the wrong you've done, He changed His mind. If so, you are not alone. Many people feel distant from God, and they are convinced they have angered Him. These feelings are not based on the truth. They come as the result of judging ourselves according to our own poor performance. If God's plans were limited to perfect people, He would have never been able to use anybody.

The Bible is full of examples of people who made mistakes and were still used mightily of God. Consider these Bible heroes just to name a few: Adam committed high treason. Noah was a drunk. David was an adulterer. Rahab was a prostitute. Job went bankrupt. Moses was a murderer. Paul murdered Christians too. Jacob was a coward. Gideon was afraid. And Samson was a womanizer.

> If God's plans were limited to perfect people, He would have never been able to use anybody.

Everyone has wrongdoing in their past which should disqualify them from ever doing God's will. However, the Bible shows us over and over how God used imperfect men and women to do great things for Him. God is good at using people despite their mistakes.

Daniel 11:35

And some of those of understanding shall fall, to refine them, purify them, and make them white, until the time of the end; because it is still for the appointed time.

God knew that people who understood Him, loved Him, and served Him would fall and make mistakes. That is a negative statement, but it's also filled with encouragement. He knew we would mess up before He called us and before He saved us. He took that all into account and loved us anyway.

And now, He has a plan for each one of us that has not been thwarted or canceled.

In God's kingdom, even your mistakes prepare you for the future. According to this verse in Daniel, mistakes refine you and purify you. Living a holy life is important, and we should all strive to live a life pleasing to God. However, the truth is, we all fall short in one way or another. Yet, when God is involved, your failures can further His cause in your life instead of disqualifying you. You may have experienced a lengthy and complicated time of preparation in your life. In the process, maybe you've made some grievous errors. Take heart. Learn from them. Don't give up on the promises God has made to you. You are being refined and purified for His use. You are a work in progress, and God's will for your life is still for the appointed time.

God certainly didn't commission the sin and disobedience, but whatever you have done is not enough to stop God from accomplishing His will. He's still going to do what He said He would do in your life if you let Him. God will never give up on you, so don't you give up on Him. Be encouraged! It's not because you are so good, but because He is so good. He can bring His will to pass

> God will never give up on you, so don't you give up on Him.

in your life despite all your mistakes, and in the end, He gets all the glory.

A SECOND CHANCE FOR PETER

Many of us can identify with the apostle Peter. He was a man that loved God passionately but was also known to make mistakes. No doubt, one of the biggest regrets in Peter's life was the night he betrayed Jesus three times.

At the last supper, Jesus was preparing His disciples by warning them of what was just ahead:

Matthew 26:31-35

Then Jesus said to them, "All of you will be made to stumble because of Me this night, for it is written: 'I will strike the Shepherd, and the sheep of the flock will be scattered.' But after I have been raised, I will go before you to Galilee." Peter answered and said to Him, "Even if all are made to stumble because of You, I will never be made to stumble." Jesus said to him, "Assuredly, I say to you that this night, before the rooster crows, you will deny Me three times." Peter said to Him, "Even if I have to die with You, I will not deny You!" And so said all the disciples.

Peter had good intentions and he had a bold confession, but we all know what happened.

Matthew 26:69-75

Now Peter sat outside in the courtyard. And a servant girl came to him, saying, "You also were with Jesus of Galilee." But he denied it before them all, saying, "I do not know what you are saying." And when he had gone out to the gateway, another girl saw him and said to those who were there, "This fellow also was with Jesus of Nazareth." But again he denied with an oath, "I do not know the Man!" And a little later those who stood by came up and said to Peter, "Surely you also are one of them, for your speech betrays you." Then he began to curse and swear, saying, "I do not know the Man!" Immediately a rooster crowed. And Peter remembered the word of Jesus who had said to him, "Before the rooster crows, you will deny Me three times." So he went out and wept bitterly.

God used Peter to do great things even after such a huge mistake.

Those words are painful to read. My heart goes out to Peter. Everyone can identify with the pain Peter experienced. He was a good man who made a mistake. I'm glad he didn't quit. I'm glad he wasn't disqualified. God used Peter to do great things even after such a huge mistake.

Every Bible commentary I've read on this subject agrees that when Jesus met with the disciples on the Sea of Galilee after His resurrection, His conversation with Peter was for the purpose of restoring Peter after his betrayal. Jesus didn't want Peter to be overcome by guilt and despair and fail to fulfill his ministry. We can learn much about the heart of God from this account of restoration, and it's important that we do. Peter's account was recorded for our benefit.

John 21:15-17

So when they had eaten breakfast, Jesus said to Simon. Peter, "Simon, son of Jonah, do you love Me more than these?"

He said to Him, "Yes, Lord; You know that I love You."

He said to him, "Feed My lambs."

He said to him again a second time, "Simon, son of Jonah, do you love Me?"

He said to Him, "Yes, Lord; You know that I love You."

He said to him, "Tend My sheep."

He said to him the third time, "Simon, son of Jonah, do you love Me?"

Peter was grieved because He said to him the third time, "Do you love Me?" And he said to Him, "Lord, You know all things; You know that I love You."

Jesus said to him, "Feed My sheep."

After what Peter had done, the Lord simply asked Peter, "Do you love Me?" That is not what I would have expected. In our natural way of doing things, I can think of several questions that might be asked such as, "Are you sorry for what you've done?" "Have you learned anything from this experience?" "Do you promise to do better in the future?" "How can I ever trust you again?"

Instead, Jesus asked simply, "Do you love Me?"

Why? Because that's all that matters! Jesus asked three questions, and they were all the same, "Do you love Me?"

The natural reaction is to go back into the past and relive the worst moments of your life, grieving and feeling sadness and regret. Yet, in Peter's case and ours, it was all past tense. Jesus pulled Peter out of the past and into the present by making the main thing, the main thing.

What you've done doesn't matter. How you feel about it doesn't matter. What does matter is this: Do you love Jesus? He can overcome anything from your past. The only thing you must bring to the equation is love for Him.

Quit asking and answering the wrong questions: What went wrong? How did it happen? Why did you do it? It won't change anything. If you still love Jesus and still believe the Bible, then you're still standing, and God still has a plan for your future. You may say, "Yes, but you don't know what I've done." Did you betray Jesus three times in public? Have you cursed and sworn in front of others and insisted you don't know Him?

Notice how Jesus pulled Peter out of the past and got his attention on the present and the future. "Do you love me?" (present tense). "Feed my lambs" (future tense). "Do you love me?" (present tense). "Tend my sheep" (future tense). "Do you love me?" (present tense). "Feed my sheep" (future tense). Peter's future ministry was to feed the sheep, which he went on to do in spite of his failure. That phrase "feed my sheep" represents whatever God has called you to do.

Jesus was reassuring Peter that nothing had changed on heaven's end. He was saying to Peter, "I still love you. I still have a plan for you. I'm still going to use you." The point Jesus was making was this: "What you've done hasn't changed anything as far as I'm concerned. Has it changed you? Do you still love Me?"

Peter could have fled to a deep, dark hole of regret and sadness and never been heard from again. But Jesus rescued him by getting him into the present and having him confess the one truth that makes all the difference. "I love you, Lord Jesus!" Focus on your love for Him! Leave your sins behind and get ready for your future.

A NEW BEGINNING FOR THE PRODIGAL SON

Another example which reveals God's heart of restoration is the story of the prodigal son in Luke 15. As the account says, the younger son took all his inheritance and left home for a far country. Verse 13 tells us "...there [he] wasted his possessions with prodigal living." Things got so bad he took a job feeding hogs, and even then, he didn't earn enough to buy food. So he decided to go back home.

Luke 15:18-19

I will arise and go to my father, and will say to him, "Father, I have sinned against heaven and before you, and I am no longer worthy to be called your son. Make me like one of your hired servants."

The son had a speech prepared for his father. It was filled with contrition and regret, but the reunion didn't go as the son expected.

Luke 15:20-21

And he arose and came to his father. But when he was still a great way off, his father saw him and had compassion, and ran and fell on his neck and kissed him. And the son said to him, "Father, I have sinned against

heaven and in your sight, and am no longer
worthy to be called your son."

The son continues with his pitiful speech about the past, not recognizing what's going on around him.

Luke 15:22-24

But the father said to his servants, "Bring out
the best robe and put it on him, and put a
ring on his hand and sandals on his feet. And
bring the fatted calf here and kill it, and let
us eat and be merry; for this my son was dead
and is alive again; he was lost and is found."
And they began to be merry.

It was as if the father and the son were on two different frequencies. As the son was rehearsing his faults and failures, the father was planning a celebration. One was filled with sadness, and the other was filled with joy. The son was stuck in the past, but the father was rejoicing over the future.

Let's notice what the father did not do. He did not say, "Tell me what you've done, and don't leave anything out." He didn't say, "Have you learned anything from your mistakes?" Or "How can I ever trust you again?" That's all past tense, and he did not go there. It was time to move forward and look ahead.

Many people come to God and ruin their own party. The Father is planning a celebration for you, so don't spoil it! God is ready to go forward with His plan, which includes a plan for your life. You haven't been put on the bench or relegated to a lesser role than God's best. Get on with the program! Get out of the past and get ready for the amazing future God has for your life!

There are people waiting for you to get over the past. They are waiting for you and the Lord to get on the same page, with the past behind you. You don't have to deal with regrets for the rest of your life. Do you still love Him? Do you still want to do His will? Do you still have a passion for His plans for your life? You *can* go forward. He took care of everything else.

He doesn't want you to fulfill His will in your life because you're sorry about what you've done and trying to pay Him back for all your mistakes. That should never be the issue. Your motivation should be based on your love for Him. The question is not what you have done wrong and how you can make it right. That's living life with regret and trapped in the past. The truth is, you can't do enough good works to make your past right.

> Get on with the program! Get out of the past and get ready for the amazing future God has for your life!

It all comes down to the same question Jesus asked Peter: Do you love Him? If your answer is yes, then it's time to get out of the past. Get on with your future. He'll lead the way!

CHAPTER 7

THE POISON
of Unforgiveness

God is serious about forgiveness. It is one of the most important doctrines in the kingdom. Without it, we couldn't come back into fellowship with God or go to heaven, and all His plans for us would be for naught. Yet forgiveness goes beyond God forgiving us of our sins; we must also forgive others.

In order to live free from regrets, we must not only deal with past mistakes we've made, but we must also forgive past offenses others have done to us. Forgiving those who have wronged us is not always easy to do, but it is possible and necessary.

Unforgiveness is lethal—it's sin and dangerous. It affects your prayer life, and it affects your faith life. To be spiritually healthy, it must be rejected. Someone once said,

"Unforgiveness is like attempting to poison someone else by taking the poison yourself." It is far more likely that unforgiveness will harm you more than the person who did you wrong.

Jesus said in Mark 11:25:

> And whenever you stand praying, if you have **anything** against **anyone**, forgive him, that your Father in heaven may also forgive you your trespasses.

What do we have to forgive? Anything. Who do we have to forgive? Anyone. This topic is so important that you should stop for a moment and check your heart. If you have *anything* against *anyone*, the Lord made it very clear that you must forgive them. This is not optional! Many Christians today are suffering with resentment and regret because they harbor unforgiveness and ill will toward others.

Unforgiveness is lethal—it's sin and dangerous.

Jesus would never tell you to do something you could not do. He also would never tell you to do something that He was not willing to do. In fact, Jesus is the greatest example of forgiveness in the history of the world. No one was treated worse than Jesus or forgave more than Jesus, and He expects you and me to follow His example (Ephesians 5:2). Freely we have received, so freely we give.

> No one was treated worse than Jesus or forgave more than Jesus, and He expects you and me to follow His example

Many people today are making themselves miserable because they're out to get justice. They've been wronged, and they won't be happy until they get justice. In most cases, people would be a lot happier if they would *give forgiveness* instead of *demanding justice*. Justice isn't always possible because it requires other people to cooperate, which can be a long process that leads nowhere. On the other hand, you can always give forgiveness. It puts you in charge and gives you power, and you don't need anyone's cooperation. Bottom line, getting justice is *sometimes* necessary, but giving forgiveness *always* works.

You may have been hurt so badly or done so wrong by others that you feel as if you just cannot let it go. Or, maybe you've never tried to forgive, or you've tried and failed. I have good news for you. You can do it! The answer is in God's Words.

Jesus shared the parable of the unforgiving servant to illustrate why we should be willing to forgive.

Matthew 18:23-33

Therefore the kingdom of heaven is like a certain king who wanted to settle accounts with his servants. And when he had begun to settle accounts, one was brought to him who owed him ten thousand talents. But as he was not able to pay, his master commanded that he be sold, with his wife and children and all that he had, and that payment be made. The servant therefore fell down before him, saying, "Master, have patience with me, and I will pay you all." Then the master of that servant was moved with compassion, released him, and forgave him the debt. But that servant went out and found one of his fellow servants who owed him a hundred denarii; and he laid hands on him and took him by the throat, saying, "Pay me what you owe!" So his fellow servant fell down at his feet and begged him, saying, "Have patience with me, and I will pay you all." And he would not, but went and threw him into prison till he should pay the debt. So when his fellow servants saw what had been done, they were very grieved, and came and told their master all that had been done. Then his master, after he had called him, said to him, "You wicked servant! I forgave you all that debt because you begged me. Should you not also have had

*compassion on your fellow servant, just as I
had pity on you?"*

It's so easy to get our eyes on what happened to us, how badly we were treated, and how it made us feel. But this parable gives us a look at forgiveness through God's eyes. After seeing forgiveness from His perspective and knowing firsthand the many sins God has forgiven us of, we should be willing to forgive anyone of anything.

When Jesus began to teach His disciples this New Testament doctrine of forgiveness, it was different than anything they had ever heard. They knew about the blood of animals being offered to cover the sins of the nation under the old covenant, but when it came to relating to other people, it was an eye for an eye, a tooth for a tooth, and so on.

They were shocked when Jesus said this in Luke 17:4:

> *And if he* [your brother] *sins against you
> seven times in a day, and seven times in a
> day returns to you, saying, "I repent," you
> shall forgive him.*

They had never heard anything like that before. No other religion they knew of had such high standards. In verse 5, they immediately replied, *"Lord, increase our faith."*

Forgiving someone seven times in one day was almost more than they could bear. I can just imagine Peter trying to wrap his head around this new thought: Seven times? If my brother sins against me, I must forgive him seven times. It's not five times or six times but seven times! No other religion must live up to such a standard, but the Lord said it. So, seven times it is. Maybe he was thinking that on the eighth time he was free to get even and give the person what they deserved.

Peter came to Jesus to discuss this topic again as if he had finally accepted this new "seven-times rule."

Matthew 18:21-22

Then Peter came to Him and said, "Lord, how often shall my brother sin against me, and I forgive him? Up to seven times?"

Jesus said to him, "I do not say to you, up to seven times, but up to seventy times seven."

The number just increased from seven to four hundred and ninety! Religion always wants a number or a rule to qualify and quantify every act, but Jesus' emphasis wasn't on the number at all. Jesus point was all about forgiveness. When Peter put his attention on the number, Jesus gave him a number that could never be met.

The point is, there is no limit to God's forgiveness toward us, and therefore, there should be no limit to our forgiveness toward others. If God had given us a number of times He would forgive us but no more, we probably would have exceeded it and gone to hell. Thank God for His limitless forgiveness. This is how the kingdom works: God forgives us, and we forgive others.

Jesus said in John 15:18:

> *If the world hates you, you know that it hated*
> *Me before it hated you.*

Unfortunately, we live in a world where we can be hated, cursed, attacked, and persecuted for doing good. In this climate, bad things can happen to good people, so learning to forgive and practice forgiveness is crucial. Without the power of forgiveness operating in our lives, it would be possible—even easy—to grow hard and cold and live a life filled with bitterness and regret.

If you're thinking, *I want to forgive. I know I should, but I don't know if I can.* Then here's good news. Jesus gave you and I practical teaching that will help anyone who's struggling with unforgiveness.

Matthew 5:43

You have heard that it was said, "You shall
love your neighbor and hate your enemy."

This was a Jewish tradition commonly held in that day. It really doesn't take any effort to love your friends and hate your enemies. Although the Old Testament did not teach this, it was practiced and believed. So, as Jesus said, the people had heard this saying. In the next verse, Jesus does away

This is how the kingdom works: God forgives us, and we forgive others.

with this tradition and lifts the standard higher than ever before. He will also show us how to get free from unforgiveness and forgive anyone who has wronged us. He puts this vital, practical advice in one verse with three parts.

Matthew 5:44

(Part 1) *But I say to you, love your enemies, bless those who curse you...*

Jesus begins by mentioning the lowest level of offense. If someone chooses to be your enemy and curses you, Jesus tells you to bless them anyway. Think about it: They curse. We bless. That right there may be enough to ward off unforgiveness. Don't talk about what they said and how wrong it was—just bless them. If that's not enough to keep you from harboring unforgiveness, you may need to go to the next level.

(Part 2) *...do good to those who hate you...*

If you have people in your life who hate you and the very mention of their names causes resentment to rise up in you, take matters into your own hands and do good to them. You certainly may not feel like doing a favor for someone who hates you, but you will feel the positive impact more than they will. Of course, these steps must be taken in faith. The objective is not to be a doormat and let people walk all over you but to break the power of unforgiveness in your life. Doing good to those who hate you is an act of faith that produces victory in you. It may or may not change the other person, but it can be the key that sets you free.

Finally, when all else fails in the most difficult cases, Jesus reveals the greatest weapon in the world to use against unforgiveness. The weapon is prayer.

> **(Part 3)** ...*and pray for those who spitefully use you and persecute you.*

There are times in life when you are hurt so badly your pain can't be put into words. There is no way to undo what was done or make it right. If that's where you are right now and nothing else has brought relief, I can tell you that prayer will. If you will take time to really pray for the offender, the pain will subside, the anger will diminish, and the unforgiveness will eventually go away.

Begin by telling God you forgive the person. You may not feel like forgiving them but say it by faith. Then lift up the person to God and ask Him to forgive them. Pray that the person's eyes are opened and that they find and do the will of God in their lives. Ask God to help them be fruitful and successful and bring glory to Him. As you release the love of God in you through prayer, it will begin to work in your mind and emotions. By praying for them, you will get the supernatural power of God involved in the situation, and it will overcome. I've done this, and it works! If it doesn't happen in a day or a week, don't get discouraged and quit. If you persist in prayer, it will work!

Think about Jesus. When Jesus was being crucified by people who hated Him, He prayed, "Father, forgive them for they know not what they do." Think of Stephen. He was being stoned simply because people didn't like what he preached, but his last words on earth were spoken in prayer for his enemies:

Acts 7:60

Then he knelt down and cried out with a loud voice, "Lord, do not charge them with this sin." And when he had said this, he fell asleep.

If Jesus and Stephen could forgive those who tortured and put them to death without cause, we can forgive those who do us wrong. God is greater than the devil, love is greater than hate, and the power of forgiveness is greater than the power of unforgiveness. Your future is too important to be limited by harboring unforgiveness from past experiences. Give forgiveness a chance and put your past behind you once and for all.

CHAPTER 8

BROKEN
Relationships

Another one of life's experiences that can cause regret is the area of broken relationships. We can all agree that broken relationships are real life events that cause real pain. It hurts to lose friends, and the truth is, it's going to happen to all of us at one time or another. There's no getting around it. Most of us don't want to hurt anyone and we don't want to get hurt, but it happens just the same. This area caught me off guard more than any other since I became a Christian.

Now, most people know that when they get saved and give their life to God, they will lose some relationships. They are prepared to do so even if they lose some friends who don't understand their new lifestyle and criticize it.

1 Peter 4:4 (NLT)

*Of course, your former friends are surprised
when you no longer plunge into the flood of
wild and destructive things they do. So they
slander you.*

Most of us have lost friends in the world because of our
faith in God, and we realize this is part of the price we pay
to follow Jesus. But, sooner or later, we make new Christian
friends who share our values and our love for the Lord. If you
go into the ministry like I have, you make ministry friends as
well who share your vision and are headed the same direc-
tion, walking the same path. I think most of us have the idea
that we will keep these Christian friends for life. So it can
come as a big surprise that in some instances, that's just
not the case. If you live in the kingdom long enough, you're
going to lose friends. That may not be considered a "precious promise," but it's the truth.

Let me explain it this way. Not every Christian relationship you have will last a lifetime. You might as well be
prepared for it. Over the course of your Christian life, you
will make friends, and you will lose friends. I won't discuss
how to win friends and influence people in this book; there's
plenty of material available on that already. But I will discuss
how to lose friends. I'm not sure I've ever seen a book on
that.

Bottom line, if you don't learn how to let a broken relationship go, it can be a cause of grief and regret that you'll

never get over. The first step to freedom is to realize that it does happen and understanding this means that you won't be so surprised when it happens to you. The apostle Paul cautioned us about this very thing in the book of Romans.

Romans 12:18

If it is possible, as much as depends on you,
live peaceably with all men.

Did you notice that Paul didn't say to live peaceably with all men? That's just not possible. There are some relationships that just won't work out, and they won't be long term. What Paul did say was to do your best to get along with everybody. If you're a troublemaker or a lousy friend, this chapter is not for you. I'm not trying to make excuses for Christians who can't get along with anyone. This chapter is for people who are doing their best to serve God, but they have lost relationships in the process.

In verse 18, Paul said to get along "if it is possible...." Sometimes you've done your best to save a relationship, and it's not possible. Paul also said "...as much as depends on you...." If it was only up to you, then you could salvage every relationship. But some things are out of your control because the other person has something to say about it.

A split between friends can come for many reasons. It may be your fault because of what you've done or said. Maybe there's nothing you can do to make it right. Or maybe it's their fault because of something they did or said, or it's a

Some relationships are seasonal and mutually beneficial for a time, but when the season is over, it's best for both parties to move on.

combination of the two. Nevertheless, try as you might, there is no reconciliation. It's possible that God is wanting to move you out of a relationship that will hinder you and, ultimately, hold you back. Some relationships are seasonal and mutually beneficial for a time, but when the season is over, it's best for both parties to move on.

Listen to me. Don't apply this to your spouse. If you're having marriage problems, special care needs to be taken, including counseling and prayer. The subject we are dealing with here has to do with friends, employers, employees, partners, and associates in life. Don't apply these principles to your marriage. Don't you leave your spouse, and say I told you to do it. Go talk to your pastor and get help.

Look with me at Paul's writing in Romans 12:18 once again:

If it is possible, as much as depends on you,
live peaceably with all men.

While Paul didn't say outrightly to move on if you do your best to live peaceably and can't reconcile a friendship, but it is implied. It's important to establish this because some people's pasts are littered with broken relationships that have scarred them and continue to rob them of peace, joy, and confidence. They are relationships that are broken beyond repair and will never be fixed in this life. If that's you, decide to move on. You must stop wasting time and emotional energy on things that will never change. Let it go! Get on with what God has for you.

Success in life is not determined by how many friends you have. Of course, it's important to have friends and maintain relationships, but you don't have to be lifelong friends with everyone you know. When you lose a friend or a relationship, it's not the worst thing in the world. It's better to be the friend of God, no matter how many relationships it costs. When you stand before God, He's not going to ask how many friends you had? He is going to ask, "Did you do what I called you to do?"

It's impossible for you to hang on to every person and every relationship you've ever had in your life. Don't put yourself under that kind of pressure. Some friendships and relationships aren't going to last, and that's okay.

One of the best examples of a servant of God we have in the Bible is Paul. Let's look at an account of friendship in his life. After spending some time back home following one of the most successful missionary journeys of all time, Paul approached Barnabus, his companion and travel partner, to plan another missions trip.

Acts 15:36

Then after some days Paul said to Barnabas, "Let us now go back and visit our brethren in every city where we have preached the word of the Lord, and see how they are doing."

In Acts 13, Paul and Barnabus had specifically been called out by name and sent out together by God as apostles to the Gentile world. They were the original dynamic duo. Together they traveled, saw miracles, preached, suffered persecution, and planted the New Testament church in the Gentile world. With such a supernatural history, you might think they would never go their separate ways, but you would be wrong.

Acts 15:37-41

Now Barnabas was determined to take with them John called Mark. But Paul insisted that they should not take with them the one who had departed from them in Pamphylia, and had not gone with them to the work. Then the contention became so sharp that they parted from one another. And so Barnabas took Mark and sailed to Cyprus; but Paul chose Silas and departed, being commended by the brethren to the grace of God. And he went through Syria and Cilicia, strengthening the churches.

Mark was Barnabus' nephew. He had gone on the first missionary journey and left Paul and Barnabus before the trip was over. Paul had no tolerance for quitters. He refused to allow Mark to come on the next journey, and Barnabus insisted that he do so. It says, "The contention became so sharp that they parted from one another." The word *sharp* in the Greek means *furious anger.* They had a fight, and they were angry with each other! Paul and Barnabus had a disagreement on a minor issue, and the greatest missionary team of all time split up. These are Bible heroes. Aren't they just supposed to live in a spirit of love and unity all the time with angels singing in the background? No, they're just like you and me.

Couldn't somebody do something? Could Peter or John have gotten involved and helped them work it out? Our natural reaction is one of surprise and horror. How could they do this? Whose fault was it? Let's assign blame, get an apology, and work this out. I've read this passage repeatedly to see who's at fault. Who did the Bible side with? Who did wrong, and who did right? Who needs to apologize to whom? You know what, it's not there.

We can learn a lot about parting ways and moving on by the way the Bible deals with this situation. No side is taken, nothing is implied, nothing is insinuated. The Word says they had a disagreement, and they both took new partners and went their separate ways preaching the gospel. Period. There was no blame, no recovery time, no cool-down period, no counseling. They just moved on. That's great advice when relationships fail. Quit trying to ride a dead horse!

Many times, we cannot see from God's perspective. When we look from a human point of view, we see division pure and simple. We don't like division, and we try to avoid it. But in Acts 15, from a kingdom standpoint, there was one team of two men who traveled and impacted the world. After the separation, there were two teams of two men. That's not division—that's multiplication! We can't be sure whether God was for or against this split because the Bible doesn't say. What we do know is that the gospel was still being preached, the world was still being reached, and God was still being glorified.

Don't read too much into the fact that some relationships don't last. God can help you recover from anything, no matter who did what to whom. But you will put your life on hold by focusing too much over broken relationships that can't be fixed. Some relationships won't be restored until we get to heaven, and that's okay. If it's over, say your goodbyes and move on with no regrets. You will have all of eternity to spend with them when this life through.

Paul and Barnabus had a disagreement on a minor issue, and the greatest missionary team of all time split up.

CHAPTER 9

LEARNING
to Let Go

You've probably heard the saying "all is fair in love and war," but actually, it is not true at all. Sometimes love and relationships are pretty unfair—even painful. We were never promised a life free from pain or challenges. We must be prepared for whatever comes. Life isn't a game we play to see who can have the most fun. We are in a war, and in war there are casualties. War has unexpected outcomes like the loss of friends and relationships that can be messy and complicated. Relationships are lost in war and in life. Just because you've lost a friend or associate, doesn't mean you have done anything wrong or that you're getting what you deserve.

Some people are friends for a particular season in your life. They are seasonal friends because work or school or location have brought you together temporarily. When that season is over, so is the relationship. There is nothing wrong with that, and there is no need to waste time wondering why it isn't like it used to be. Things have changed, and it's okay to move on.

Some people are happy to be your friend as long as they have more money or success than you have. But as you begin to prosper or get promoted, the dynamic changes, and they may allow jealousy and envy to enter in. You may not realize what is happening except that they are becoming irritable and short-tempered with you, and there is a strain when you are together that wasn't there before. Your feelings for them may not have changed at all, but if they have allowed themselves to become jealous of your success, there may be nothing you can do to fix it. It may be time for you to move on. At first it may seem like a terribly painful thing to do but ending a relationship may be better for both of you. It's better than trying to maintain something that could produce strife and hard feelings every time you're together for years to come.

I'm not trying to be negative and discouraging. But I've not heard much teaching on this subject, and some of these things need to be said. My purpose is to help you fulfill God's will in your life by helping you get free from unnecessary weights. I'm not encouraging you to be hard to get along with and lose all your friends. But I believe that while some people consider these things, they need permission to make the difficult decision to end counterproductive relationships. They need to realize that it's okay to end a friendship rather than waste time and energy because of an unwarranted sense of obligation.

Another situation that causes relationships to change is unrealistic expectations. When you're young, you're primarily held accountable for the things you do. When you do right you benefit, and all is well. When you do wrong, you face the consequences. But the older you get, the more you're held accountable by friends and relatives for what you don't do. Pastors are especially familiar with unrealistic expectations. God bless pastors!

I had an experience with an old friend that didn't go well because of what I didn't do. The person was offended by something they thought I should have done. Life is hard enough when you're focused on what you know you're supposed to do, but it gets really complicated when people start to pass judgments based on what you didn't do.

Friends may think they know what you should do even though it's not written, required, or part of your job description. People can place their own unrealistic expectations on you because you're a relative, a Christian, a preacher, or whatever title applies to you. If you don't live up to their expectations, they can become offended even though you may not even know why. You cannot and will not make everybody happy.

I had no idea this person was offended over an incident that happened years earlier. Without going into details, let me just say when a distressful situation occurred, the person expected me to respond in a certain way. Because I didn't do what they thought I should, they were offended. I had no knowledge of this for several years. By the time they vented their frustration in an angry letter, the situation was long over. At that point, there was nothing I could do or say to change it. The person was inconsolable. Eventually, I had to make a choice. I could feel sad and remorseful and spend time, emotion, and effort trying to make things better, which probably would not have worked. Or, I could move on. I chose to move on.

You and I only have so much emotional capital to invest. Use it wisely. I am tempted to this day to feel sadness and sorrow over this experience. If I had it to do over, I would have done what they expected me to do just because they were friends. But I cannot go back. Now, it's over and so is the friendship. I look forward to the day we can be close friends again in heaven, but until then, I have work to do. I refuse to allow the enemy to limit my future with regrets from my past. The scriptures listed in the last chapter of this book have helped me move on from situations like this with supernatural joy. They can help you too!

Bottom line, these things happen. You may not be able to avoid broken relationships, but you can control how you react to them. Satan would like to use the pain associated with lost friendships to hold you back and keep you focused on the past. He wants you continually wondering if you could have done something or said something to avoid a falling out. He knows feelings of pain and regret can haunt you and limit your faith.

If you've attempted to restore fellowship with someone, and it's just not going to happen, you need to move on. Life is too short and there's too much to do to get caught up in trying to fix something that can't be fixed. There are some relationships that will not be reconciled this side of

Satan would like to use the pain associated with lost friendships to hold you back and keep you focused on the past.

heaven. The good news is that when we get to heaven, Jesus will make everything right.

Some relationships require too much from you. They are not worth the investment of time and effort required to maintain them. I'm not saying someone isn't valuable or isn't a good person. Yet, just because someone is good, valuable, and loves God doesn't mean they have to be your lifelong friend. You must decide to move on without some people. Again, it's not a pleasant experience, but it's necessary in some situations. I don't think these things are discussed much in our culture, but they should be.

There was a famous entertainer who had an expensive game room in his house, and it was told that a plaque on the wall read, "When life is over, he who has the most toys wins." That's just wrong. I think some people believe another variation which says, "When life is over, he who has the most friends wins." That, too, is wrong. Life is not a popularity contest. We are here to serve God and do His will whether anyone else likes us or not.

Jesus said He was hated, and people will hate you; a servant is not above his master. If that's true, and it is, then you shouldn't feel like it's the end of the world when someone hates you or turns against you. That's true even if it's someone who used to love you. Don't be guilty of trying to hold on to someone when it's time to let go. Trust God for the future, for new relationships, and for new friends who will help you get where you're supposed to go. Don't allow what happened in the past to limit your future.

There was a time in my life years ago, when I lost some relationships that were very important to me. As I moved from one season of life and ministry to another, there were some friendships that just couldn't continue. There was nothing I could do about them. I grieved because it hurts to lose friends! As I was praying about it and wondering if there was anything I could have done differently to change the outcome, I began to tell God how important these people were in my life. I began to ask Him how I would make it without them. I finally said, "Lord, I wouldn't be where I am today without them. I don't want to give them up."

> Trust God for the future, for new relationships, and for new friends who will help you get where you're supposed to go.

Isaiah 61:2 says, "He comforts those who mourn...," and I will never forget how He comforted me that day. He used an illustration to speak to me and showed me a picture of a space shuttle lifting off. The space shuttle itself looks like a bulky airplane. To launch, it has two rocket boosters attached to its side filled with fuel. When ignited, they lift the shuttle into space. As the shuttle leaves earth's atmosphere, the boosters having completed their task, separate from the shuttle. They fall back to earth while the shuttle continues into orbit.

As I saw this image, the Spirit of God spoke this to my heart: "You're right. These relationships were very important to you. They helped you get where you are, and you wouldn't be where you are today without them. But it's time to separate from them, like the shuttle from the rocket boosters. You wouldn't have gotten where you are without them, but you can't get where you're going with them. It's time to let them go."

Until that moment, I had the impression that I was obligated to maintain every relationship I had ever had for the rest of my life. I didn't know that it's perfectly normal to gain friends and lose friends throughout life's journey. That set me free! I'm am not only able but also willing to maintain or let go of relationships at any time—no hard feelings, nothing personal, no regrets.

When it's time to move forward, it's necessary to apply the Word of God. The absolute best way to get free from the pain of broken relationships, no matter what the cause, is to go to the Word. Speaking and meditating on scriptures allows God's power to heal the wounds and drive out the pain like nothing else in the world.

Jesus already bore our grief and sorrow, and He heals the brokenhearted. Speak out or confess the following scriptures aloud and allow God's power to heal your wounds. These verses along with many others are included in the last chapter of this book.

Over time, the Word will replace the pain of broken relationships with peace and joy. As you give God's Word entrance into your heart by confession and meditation, the Word will rise up in you when old memories and sadness try to overwhelm you.

Isaiah 53:4 — *Surely He* [Jesus] *has borne our griefs and carried our sorrows.*

Psalm 147:3 — *He* [Jesus] *heals the brokenhearted and binds up their wounds.*

Romans 12:18 — *If it is possible, as much as depends on you, live peaceably with all men.*

Mark 11:25 — *And whenever you stand praying, if you have anything against anyone, forgive him, that your Father in heaven may also forgive you your trespasses.*

1 Peter 3:9 — *Not returning evil for evil or reviling for reviling, but on the contrary blessing, knowing that you were called to this, that you may inherit a blessing.*

Confession: I have done my best to do right by everyone. I have asked for forgiveness where I was wrong, and I forgive anyone who has wronged me. Therefore, I no longer allow grief and sorrow to haunt me over broken relationships. I bless everyone, and I refuse to curse anyone. I know that any relationship that I fail to restore on earth, Jesus will restore in heaven. I have no ill will toward anybody. I have no more sorrows, no more sadness, no more regrets. I am filled with the supernatural joy of the Lord and nothing and no one can take that away!

CHAPTER 10

BITTERNESS AND
the Big Picture

Hebrews 12:14-15

Pursue peace with all people, and holiness, without which no one will see the Lord: looking carefully lest anyone fall short of the grace of God; lest any root of bitterness springing up cause trouble, and by this many become defiled.

It's very easy to become bitter while living in this fallen world. Every person on earth has had to deal with the temptation to become bitter at one time or another. Many people have become corrupted by a root of bitterness, robbing them of happiness and joy. Because they have embraced

...bitterness should be rejected, resisted, and replaced with a spirit of thanksgiving and praise.

wrong thinking in this area, they are doomed to remain in a stew of anger, resentment, and regret.

Some people have used bitterness to excuse themselves from any responsibility to become productive and fruitful, let alone strive for greatness. This is a recipe for even more unhappiness. The truth is, bitterness should be rejected, resisted, and replaced with a spirit of thanksgiving and praise.

To deal properly with feelings of bitterness, we need to adjust our perspective by looking at the big picture. Since the fall of Adam everything has changed—the world is not what it should be or what it was designed to be. As a result, many things in life are not fair. Injustices abound, and in response, people allow bitterness to spring up.

God wanted fellowship with His children so much that rather than giving up on the entire creation when Adam sinned, He allowed us to be born into a fallen world. Over the centuries, people have come into the world under various circumstances. Some have been born into slavery while others are born into poverty. Some have been born into broken homes while others grew up as orphans. Some have faced abuse, famine, and disease. So many things in life are unfair that it's easy to give up and yield to resentment.

And yet, what if you had never been born at all? Life is a gift! Despite the circumstances that surrounded you at birth, today you have an opportunity to find and know God and live with Him forever. You should be grateful for the opportunity to exist under any circumstances.

God refused to allow sin to stop His plan for a family. Of course, things on earth are not perfect. Right now, sin, evil, unfairness, and injustice are taking their toll on society. But if we focus on all the things we see and hear that are unjust and unfair, it will certainly lead to bitterness, anger, and regret. Thank God, this life is not all there is. It's simply a vapor. It's like the blink of an eye compared to eternity.

James 4:14

For what is your life? It is even a vapor that appears for a little time and then vanishes away.

Because of the high price Jesus paid for your redemption, life will be as it should be soon, and it will last for all of eternity. Don't allow the things of this life to disproportionally impact your soul and lead you into bitterness and regret. No matter how hard folks try, not all problems will be solved in this life and in this current world system. But one day soon when Jesus returns, every wrong will be made right, every injustice will be reconciled, all suffering will end, and everyone will be equal in God's kingdom. Life will be as it should be, and it will be that way forevermore.

Anyone who is born into this world has an opportunity to experience God and the life He always intended for us. By seeing the big picture, we can refuse to allow feelings and thoughts of defeat and bitterness to defile our thinking. Being born into a fallen world with all its pain is better than not being born at all. We should be thankful for the gift of life and endeavor to make the most of it.

If you're angry, resentful, and filled with rage because of what life has done to you, then you're not on the right path. Instead, follow Jesus and navigate this temporary season of your existence by focusing on eternity. Because of Jesus, the best is yet to come! The apostle Paul didn't have it easy, but he was comforted by the fact that this life is followed by an eternity, which is beyond our ability to fully comprehend.

Romans 8:18

For I consider that the sufferings of this present time are not worthy to be compared with the glory which shall be revealed in us.

The glory to come is something worth waiting for, something worth living for, and even something worth dying for. Even though life is short, every life counts. No one should waste their life by giving in to bitterness.

Pastor Billy Joe Daugherty, who was my pastor in Tulsa for 19 years before he moved to heaven, often told the story of when he was just getting started in ministry. During those days, he met a very seasoned and successful preacher and asked if he had any advice.

> By seeing the big picture, we can refuse to allow feelings and thoughts of defeat and bitterness to defile our thinking.

The older minister said, "If you don't get bitter, you'll make it." From that day on, Pastor Billy Joe lived by that rule, and so should we.

BEING WRONGFULLY TREATED

One of the main causes of bitterness is being wrongfully treated by other people. You can't control what people do to you, but you can control how you respond. There is no reason to allow anyone to cause bitterness and regret in your life. You have the power to stop a root of bitterness from springing up. If it's already sprung up, you have the power to resist it and uproot it.

Paul endured great trials and persecution, but he never allowed himself to become bitter.

2 Corinthians 1:8

For we do not want you to be ignorant,
brethren, of our trouble which came to us in
Asia: that we were burdened beyond mea-
sure, above strength, so that we despaired
even of life.

In other accounts of Scripture, Paul listed his hardships as a badge of honor.

2 Corinthians 11:23-26

...in labors more abundant, in stripes above
measure, in prisons more frequently, in
deaths often. From the Jews five times I
received forty stripes minus one. Three times
I was beaten with rods; once I was stoned;
three times I was shipwrecked; a night and
a day I have been in the deep; in journeys
often, in perils of waters, in perils of robbers,
in perils of my own countrymen, in perils of
the Gentiles, in perils in the city, in perils in
the wilderness, in perils in the sea, in perils
among false brethren.

These things weren't easy to endure, but Paul accepted them as part of living life in a fallen world. We were never promised that life would be easy. The Bible tells us that challenges and temptations will come. In fact, the more you do for God, the more you will become a target for the enemy. But think about this: People who become bitter and depressed over trivial things in life, cannot be trusted to do great things for God.

Paul and Silas were beaten and put into the dungeon in Philippi for preaching the gospel (Acts 16). Rather than feeling sorry for themselves or bitter toward others, the Bible says they prayed and sang praises to God. You may endure slander and false accusations or be scorned because of your faith or hated because of your relationship with Jesus. Overcoming in those situations is just as noble as taking a city or preaching to a king.

Jesus said in Matthew 5:10-12:

> *Blessed are those who are persecuted for*
> *righteousness' sake, For theirs is the kingdom*
> *of heaven. Blessed are you when they revile*
> *and persecute you, and say all kinds of evil*
> *against you falsely for My sake. Rejoice and*
> *be exceedingly glad, for great is your reward*
> *in heaven, for so they persecuted the prophets*
> *who were before you.*

We must face the challenges that come our way, and most of the time, we don't get to choose the challenge. You may be in a situation right now you can't control or get away from. You may be asking yourself, *Why me?* or *What did I ever do to deserve this treatment?* I want to encourage you not to give in to bitterness or regret. God's Word has the answers to help you in your time of need.

Peter had a lot to say in his first epistle about being treated wrongly and how to deal with it.

1 Peter 2:19-21

For this is commendable, if because of conscience toward God one endures grief, suffering wrongfully. For what credit is it if, when you are beaten for your faults, you take it patiently? But when you do good and suffer, if you take it patiently, this is commendable before God. For to this you were called, because Christ also suffered for us, leaving us an example, that you should follow His steps.

This is not the natural way to look at suffering wrongfully. Some people are so competitive by nature, they can't let anything go. They must have the last word or get in the last lick: "If you hit me, I'll hit you back." Yet Peter tells us that when you do good and suffer and you take it patiently (and quietly), it is commendable before God.

1 Peter 2:20 (AMPC)

[After all] what kind of glory [is there in it] if, when you do wrong and are punished for it, you take it patiently? But if you bear

*patiently with suffering [which results] when
you do right and that is undeserved, it is
acceptable and pleasing to God.*

When unfair treatment comes your way, you literally have an opportunity to be pleasing to God. And when you think like this, you close the door on bitterness.

Peter reminds us that Jesus is our example, and he goes on to say 1 Peter 2:23:

> *...when He was reviled, did not revile
> in return; when He suffered, He did not
> threaten, but committed Himself to Him who
> judges righteously.*

In chapter 3, Peter continues his teaching on ill-treatment:

1 Peter 3:9

*Not returning evil for evil or reviling for
reviling, but on the contrary blessing, knowing that you were called to this, that you may
inherit a blessing.*

The Amplified Bible, Classic Edition says, "Never return evil for evil or insult for insult (scolding, tongue-lashing, berating), but on the contrary blessing...."

For sure, this is a different way of dealing with insults, scoldings, or tongue-lashings. We are to respond with blessings. We give what we have. We are born again, so we have the nature of God, the love of God, and the blessings of God abiding on the inside of us. That's the currency we trade in.

When I travel to minister in other countries, I don't always take the time to change my American dollars into the local currency. For instance, I've traveled to Tanzania in East Africa many times. Occasionally, I've gone to pay for something and been given the price in Tanzanian schillings when all I have on me is dollars. I've had to say, "I don't have any schillings today. Can I pay in U. S. dollars"? They gladly accept dollars. In fact, most people prefer them. And if that's all I have in my wallet, that's all I can give them.

When people lash out in anger, hate, and cursing, we don't have that currency. We must give the change back in blessings because we are blessed. Blessing is all we have in our wallets! This kind of response eliminates the risk of allowing a root of bitterness to spring up.

It's not a sign of weakness to overcome evil with good; it's a sign of strength. Lest you think that kindness will somehow leave you vulnerable to harm, notice what Peter goes on to say:

1 Peter 3:13-14

And who is he who will harm you if you become followers of what is good? But even if you should suffer for righteousness' sake, you are blessed. "And do not be afraid of their threats, nor be troubled."

When you choose to live life God's way, not only are you safe from bitterness and regret, but also God will protect you. He will keep you from harm. You will not need to be concerned with people's threats or let them bother you in the least. The truth is, you are not just to live free from bitterness, but you can live above it! These are powerful promises for every believer that work in the real world.

Peter sums up this teaching in chapter 4 with the following verses:

1 Peter 4:12-14

Beloved, do not think it strange concerning the fiery trial which is to try you, as though some strange thing happened to you; but rejoice to the extent that you partake of Christ's sufferings, that when His glory is revealed, you may also be glad with exceeding joy. If you are reproached for the name of Christ, blessed are you, for the Spirit of glory

...you are not just to live free from bitterness, but you can live above it!

and of God rests upon you. On their part
He is blasphemed, but on your part He is
glorified.

Peter associates gladness and joy with trials and sufferings. That's a new way to approach life. Since you only get one life to live, why waste it by yielding to bitterness and regret? Remember when times get tough, blessed are you because the Spirit of glory and the Spirit of God rest on you!

CHAPTER 11

GETTING
Over Grief

My grandfather on my mother's side of the family lived into his 90s. Everybody loved Papaw. He was a wonderful person and a very wise man. One day we were driving through the town where he had lived his entire life, and we happened to pass by the cemetery. As he looked out over the gravestones, he said matter-of-factly, "I have more friends in the cemetery than I do in town." He had outlived nearly everyone he'd grown up with.

I was much younger and had never given it much thought, but if you live long enough, you will experience the passing of friends and loved ones in this life. This is undoubtedly one of life's most painful experiences. Death is part of life, and there is no way to get around it. "…It is appointed for men to die once, but after this the judgment" (Hebrews 9:27).

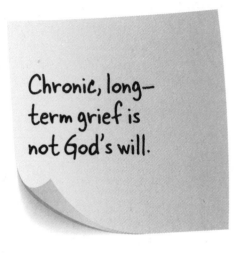

Chronic, long-term grief is not God's will.

Unfortunately, there is nothing I can say that will bring your loved ones back. The teaching here is designed to help you with the grief and mourning that comes from the loss of a loved one. I would never belittle the pain you've felt over your loss, dishonor the memory of one who has passed, or attempt to talk you out of the natural grieving process. What I want to do is help you get over the pain and agony of loss. I'm convinced it's not God's best for His people to experience crippling grief year after year over the loss of a loved one.

Chronic, long-term grief is not God's will. You *can* move on from sadness and mourning to the joy that only God can give. With God's help, you can go from sadness over a loved one's passing to joy over your heavenly reunion with them, which is closer with each day. If you will read the following words with an open mind, I believe the Lord Himself will minister healing to your broken heart.

Jesus wants you to be happy. He wants you to be free, and He paid a high price so you could be free. I'm not talking about faking joy; I'm talking about a joy that wells up from the inside. Joy is a fruit of the Spirit, a genuine gladness that is evident in your life. People should say the same about you as what was written in the Psalms.

Psalm 126:2-3

Then our mouth was filled with laughter, and our tongue with singing. Then they said among the nations, "The Lord has done great things for them." The Lord has done great things for us, and we are glad.

Jesus wants you to be happy.

Psalm 144:15

Happy are the people who are in such a state; Happy are the people whose God is the Lord!

God wants you to be happy! This is true for everyone. God does not want you to mourn the loss of a loved one for the rest of your life or live a life that's less than happy and fulfilled because of the loss. The last thing those who loved you—spouse, parents, other family, and friends—would want is for you to spend the rest of your life in sorrow over their departure. No, God wants you happy, and they would want you happy!

FIVE STEPS TO REACH FOR THE FUTURE WITH JOY

Below are five steps to help you put grief behind, so you can reach for the future with joy:

1. Realize that death was not part of God's original plan

I was speaking with a friend of many years on the one-year anniversary of his wife's death. I just happened to call him that day, and we laughed and cried together as he told me stories about her life.

I was prompted to remind him of this truth, which I believe is the one truth that allows recovery from loss to begin. It is simply this: Death was not God's plan for mankind. Death never was supposed to be part of life on earth, and God never intended for you to be separated from your loved ones in this way. He never wanted you to experience death at all.

In the beginning, we were created to live forever, and our bodies were never supposed to die. Adam's sin caused death to be part of human life, and God had nothing to do with it. God told Adam not to sin, so it's not right to blame God for something we (mankind) brought on ourselves. How can God minister to someone who believes He killed their loved one? This kind of thinking has caused many people to become bitter toward God and prevented them from fully recovering from grief and mourning.

It is very difficult to receive God's comfort and healing if you think death was His doing. I've seen people die and watched as they go through the process of passing from this world, and I can tell you that it

> Adam's sin caused death to be part of human life, and God had nothing to do with it.

helps tremendously when you know beyond any doubt that God is not responsible. It helps to know that God is on your side, and He's touched with the feeling of your infirmities. He's a very present help in time of trouble—bringing the help not the trouble.

Isaiah 61:3 says that God consoles those who mourn. Times of mourning will come, and He will be there to help, to comfort, and to heal. It's the thief that comes to steal, kill, and destroy.

You may wonder, *How long should I mourn over a loved one's passing?* I can't answer that, and I don't think anybody can answer that. There are many factors involved: How close was this person to you, how long did you know the person, or how long were you together. How did they pass away? God understands that we go through seasons of mourning, but it isn't His will for you to mourn for the rest of your life.

Don't believe the lie that because of a loss in your life you will never be happy again.

Isaiah 61:3

To console those who mourn in Zion, to give them beauty for ashes, the oil of joy for mourning, the garment of praise for the spirit of heaviness; that they may be called trees of righteousness, the planting of the LORD, that He may be glorified.

At some point, the season of mourning needs to be followed by joy. You need to understand there's beauty on the other side of ashes, and there's joy on the other side of mourning. There's a garment of praise after the spirit of heaviness. God never said we wouldn't go through periods of grief and mourning, but we shouldn't stay there. We must allow Jesus to come and heal us, so we can move forward.

The enemy will put these thoughts in your mind to keep you from getting over grief: *I'll never be happy again. I'll never be full of joy again. I'll never be the same again.* These are lies that the enemy uses to keep people in bondage. Don't allow these thoughts to keep you trapped in an endless cycle of sadness and sorrow. Instead, quote the promises of God and let Him give you the oil of joy for mourning and the garment of praise for the spirit of heaviness. Jesus is the Healer of the brokenhearted.

2. Stop asking why

One of the reasons some people struggle to recover from the loss of a loved one is they refuse to stop asking why. The natural tendency when going through any tragedy is to ask why the tragedy happened. If you're a Christian, you may be asking God why someone you loved passed away. In many cases, you may not get that answer in this life. That may not be something you want to hear, but it's true.

Let's deal with the subject of why—not why the person passed away but why we won't always understand why. First of all, we don't know everything. The apostle Paul said, "We know in part..." (1 Corinthians 13:9). Later in the same chapter, Paul said in verse 12 (KJV):

> *For now we see through a glass, darkly; but then face to face: now I know in part; but then shall I know even as also I am known.*

There are many things we just won't know or understand in this life. The truth is, knowing why something happened doesn't heal our broken heart in and of itself anyway. Only Jesus can do that! Jesus can heal you even if you don't know

One of the reasons some people struggle to recover from the loss of a loved one is they refuse to stop asking why.

why it happened. Verse 12 says, "We will know even as we are known," and sometimes knowing that we will know someday has to be enough.

One day, you will be in heaven with Jesus, and He will explain things to you. When He does, you will say, "Oh! I understand. So, you are a good God, and your Word is true. You were not to blame for my troubles on earth." This is what it means to live by faith. Faith is believing in what you cannot see, and it's also believing in what you cannot understand. It may sound difficult, but you can fill in the unknowns in your life with faith.

God is not on trial. He is everything He said He is, and we should never blame God for situations we don't understand. He deserves our trust and faith in Him even in the midst of a painful situation that we do not understand and cannot explain. God doesn't go around defending Himself and explaining why everything happened to everybody to our satisfaction, even though sometimes I wish He would. He expects us to put our faith in His Word above anything we can see or feel. Believing God and His Word in the midst of tragedy and loss is just as much an act of faith as believing for salvation or divine healing.

My wife, Carol, is a testimony to the fact that God can heal a broken heart even if you don't understand why a tragedy happened. Many years ago, she was married to Christian man named Wes, and they were a young family with three small girls. They had been on a road trip visiting family and were returning to their home in Louisiana.

Carol was driving their minivan late at night, and she went to sleep at the wheel. When she awoke, the van had lost control and was flipping down the interstate. When it came to a stop, her husband and middle daughter eventually died as a result. She was left to return home a widow with two small children. She was devastated and felt broken beyond repair. The guilt and pain were nearly more than she could bear.

In the months and years to come, the Lord did a miracle in her life. He healed her broken heart and set her free from the pain and guilt that had nearly destroyed her life. Today, she is without a doubt one of the happiest people I have ever known. If you met her, you would never guess she has been through such a tragedy. When God undertakes a restoration project, He does a great job! Her testimony is included in chapter 12 where she gives more details of her recovery.

In her testimony she makes this statement: "I could not even begin the healing process until I stopped asking why." Then she gives the scripture that helped her let go and trust the Lord.

Deuteronomy 29:29

*The secret things belong to the Lord our God,
but those things which are revealed belong to
us and to our children....*

Some things are secret, and they belong to God. It's not because He cannot communicate with you; it's because He knows what's best for you. Knowing why won't bring someone back, and it is not necessary for you to be healed. If you don't know why, it may be time to quit asking. Put "the why" on the shelf, and don't think about it again. Let the Healer begin to heal your broken heart.

Another verse that God used in Carol's recovery is Jeremiah 30:17:

> *I will restore health to you and heal you of*
> *your wounds.*

Wounds can be emotional as well as physical, and emotional wounds can be even more devastating than physical ones. But God can heal you of any kind of wound and restore you spirit, soul, and body. Jesus is a wonderful Healer who is ready and willing to take you through the season of mourning and turn your sorrows into joy.

3. Understand your loved ones don't want to come back

Every testimony I've ever read or heard from anyone who's been to heaven and come back had one thing in common: they didn't want to come back. It has been a tremendous encouragement for me to imagine my loved ones in heaven knowing they are so happy they wouldn't come back if they had the chance. We shouldn't spend the rest of our lives feeling sorry for them if they are so happy they wouldn't want to be anywhere else.

I've been to many places over the years in my travels. I've been to nice places and not so nice places. I've been to some pretty awesome places, but I've never been anywhere so nice that I was willing to stay forever and never go home again to my house, or to see my family and friends. It's difficult to imagine a place so incredible you want to stay forever and never return home. That's because heaven *is* home! It's what you've been looking for; it's where you were born to be.

So many times when we mourn and become overwhelmed with sadness and grief, it's because we're looking through an earthly lens. We don't see the big picture. There's more than just this life on earth; there is life after this one in a place called heaven. We shouldn't allow an experience that ultimately makes our loved ones so happy to make us so sad. The last thing our loved ones would want is for us to live our lives in sorrow because they went to heaven.

It's also not right to compress the memory of a loved one's relationship with you into the last few weeks or months of their life on earth. Many times, we do this because we've just been through the heart-wrenching experience of watching them go home to heaven. It's the most vivid in our minds, especially if there was illness and suffering toward the end. If this person was a spouse,

> The last thing our loved ones would want is for us to live our lives in sorrow because they went to heaven.

> One of the things that makes heaven so heavenly is that our loved ones are there waiting for us.

a relative, a parent, or longtime friend, you had many good years with them. Don't disregard all the good years you had together because they may have suffered toward the end. Remember the happy times and the good days because I can promise you, that's what they're remembering. Our loved ones in heaven are not grieving over their homegoing. They have no more sadness, no more sorrow, no more regrets, and neither should you.

4. Honor your loved one's life by celebrating your reunion

We aren't talking here about getting over the person—just the pain. We aren't trying to forget them or ignore the fact that they lived. Jesus can heal you of the pain while you continue to honor their memory. We can honor their lives by remembering the good times we had with them and all the good things they did and said, and we can also honor them by celebrating our coming reunion in heaven.

One of the things that makes heaven so heavenly is that our loved ones are there waiting for us. They will be there to greet us! God recognizes those connections we have made with family and friends on earth, and He honors those connections. He loves the fact that you have people in your life you love and people who love you.

We need to go ahead and let the Lord heal us and go forward celebrating the fact that our reunion is surely coming. It's closer than it's ever been! Someday you also will pass over to the other side. If you've made Jesus Lord of your life, you have the assurance that when life on earth is over, you will go to heaven. You will be with Jesus and see God your Father face to face, and you will celebrate a glorious family reunion with all those who have gone before you. What a day that will be!

The Bible says we are surrounded by a great cloud of witnesses (Hebrews 12:1). This large crowd of saints in the grandstands of heaven includes the people you know and love who are cheering for you now. No doubt, they will be gathered together to welcome you home when you enter through the gates of heaven. That's something to look forward to and rejoice over! This is part of the good news that's so good that the bad news doesn't matter. No matter how bad it seems down here, the day is coming when you will go to heaven to be with Jesus and those you love forever and ever! I don't know about your past, but if you're a Christian, I know about your future. It's out of this world!

You may be reading this thinking, *I don't know if my loved one went to heaven. How can I deal with that?* The answer is you're right—you don't know. You aren't the judge. I'm convinced there are many people no one thought would make it who will be in heaven waiting for us. No one knows what goes on in a person's heart on their deathbed as they hover between life and death. They may appear unconscious to the outside world, but their spirits are still active and capable of communicating with God.

I'm convinced that many people make their peace with God when they may appear unconscious to us and unaware of their surroundings. I believe one of the most asked questions in heaven will be, "What are you doing here?" It will be asked of many people that no one expected to make it to heaven! You may be one of those people who is asked by everyone else, "How did you get here?" Only God knows the heart, and He's not willing that any should perish. He's giving people every opportunity to accept Jesus right up to the end. Only in heaven will we know how many deathbed conversions have resulted in eleventh-hour salvations when it seemed all hope was gone.

5. Allow the Healer to heal your broken heart

When someone is hurting, the natural tendency is to put up walls to protect and guard against pain. Some people retreat to this place of isolation and choose never to love again, never to be vulnerable again, never to hope again, and never to live again. Some people even believe they can never be happy again. There is a better way! Let the Healer mend your heart.

Psalm 147:3

*He heals the brokenhearted and binds up
their wounds.*

In the natural, it may be true that you never totally get over certain events from your past. But there is more than the natural; there is the supernatural. There is a God who can heal your broken heart. He can remove the pain without removing the memories. He can literally take the pain out of the past. It's a miracle! It's a miracle just as much as the new birth, the baptism of the Holy Spirit, and divine healing. God is the God of miracles, and He's able to heal emotions. You must let down the walls to let the Healer in. So, let go of the pain, the sadness, and the sorrow, and let Him do a miracle in your soul.

Jesus paid the price for you to be whole spirit, soul, and body. The chastisement of your peace (whatever was necessary for your peace) was upon Him. He bore your griefs and carried your sorrows, which is just as real and available as the fact that He was wounded for your transgressions and bruised for your iniquities (Isaiah 53:4-5). If you have accepted Jesus' offer to forgive your sins, why not accept His offer to take away your grief and sorrow?

You can use Psalm 30:10-12 as your own personal prayer. Begin by asking Him to help you.

Psalm 30:10

*Hear, O Lord, and have mercy on me; Lord,
be my helper!"*

He is a very present help in time of need. His eyes are on the righteous, and His ears are open to your prayers. He is touched with the feeling of your infirmities, and He understands your pain. He is ready to help. Tell Him you will trust Him to heal your broken heart and ask Him to help you. Then trust Him to do what only He can do.

In Luke 4:18, Jesus said, "He has sent me to heal the brokenhearted." No one else has ever made that claim. The surgeon can't heal a broken heart, nor can the psychiatrist. But Jesus is able and willing! Begin trusting Him now—even before the pain is gone. While you're still dealing with the sadness and sorrow of a broken heart, read the rest of this passage below and make it your own confession.

Psalm 30:11-12

*You have turned for me my mourning into
dancing; You have put off my sackcloth and
clothed me with gladness, to the end that my
glory may sing praise to You and not be silent.
O Lord my God, I will give thanks to You
forever.*

You weren't meant to live a life filled with regret. The world is waiting for you to be all that God has called you to be. People need you to rise up and overcome the events of your past. Expect God to turn your mourning into dancing and to clothe you with gladness. Reject the lie that you'll never be happy again. You can be better than you've ever been!

I have included my wife's testimony in the next chapter. Carol is living proof that God can heal the brokenhearted. As you read on, it is our desire that you will be convinced beyond all doubt that what God has done in her life, He will do in your life.

If you have accepted Jesus' offer to forgive your sins, why not accept His offer to take away your grief and sorrow?

CHAPTER 12

CAROL'S
Testimony:

HEALING FOR THE BROKENHEARTED
By Carol Fritz

In June 1989, one week before my youngest daughter's first birthday, our family was in a tragic car accident. We were on vacation in New Mexico to visit our relatives and attend my brother's wedding. My husband, Wes, and I lived in Alexandria, Louisiana, where he was stationed in the U.S. Air Force. It had been at least a year since we had seen our relatives, so there was much to catch up on.

There was also so much to do to get ready for the wedding after a very long drive. The drive took about 21 hours with the speed limit of the day, and we were traveling with three children under five, Charlotte, Laura, and LeeAnn. But we joyfully started helping with the wedding reception preparations as soon as we arrived. Whether it was wedding fun or just catching up with loved ones, there was not much rest. We averaged about five hours of sleep each night.

The sun was setting all too soon as we said our goodbyes and headed back to Louisiana. Our plan was to drive all night so most of the trip would be while the little ones were asleep. Heading east on I-40, my job was simply to drive as long as I could then wake up Wes. He would drive most of the way back to Alexandria. Our oldest daughter, Charlotte, was riding up front with me in our Toyota van. Wes and Laura were lying in the back, and our youngest was in her car seat. Laura asked for a sip of my root beer and settled in to sleep.

It didn't take long for my eyes to get really heavy after everyone else fell asleep. Mile after mile, it was a constant struggle for me to stay awake. I cranked up the music as loud as I could without stirring anyone but to no avail. Suddenly, I found myself waking up as the van was driving through the rough median. I woke up screaming, "We're wrecking!" Suddenly and quickly, the van went from rough riding to spinning and rolling. Charlotte and I were screaming as we found ourselves in the ditch on the opposite side of the interstate.

I checked Charlotte for injuries, and there seemed to be none at the time. We unbuckled ourselves and went to find the rest of the family. Shockingly, there was no one at all in the backseat when we landed, including almost one-year-old LeeAnn, who had been buckled in her car seat. She was the first one we found. She was sitting up on the edge of the blacktop crying. There was a lot of blood coming from a couple of glass cuts on her head. My mother-in-law, Bev, was an emergency

Suddenly and quickly, the van went from rough riding to spinning and rolling.

medical technician (EMT), and she had taught the family what to do if ever there was a wreck. I did what she had taught us both for Charlotte and LeeAnn. When I had completely checked and cleared LeeAnn for major injuries, I picked her up. Charlotte was by my side helping.

By that time, a trucker was approaching the scene. He stopped, jumped out of his truck, and said that he had radioed for help.

"The police and ambulance are on the way!" he said.

His headlights lit up the scene, and together we saw what happened to Wes and Laura. They were both lying in a large puddle of their own blood. It seemed like Laura was dead, but Wes was breathing weirdly. I knew that touching them in any way would only harm them. The scene populated fast. I guarded the two on the ground like a momma bear. Well meaning, untrained people can hurt those in such a vulnerable state. The trucker helped me as I had explained all that I knew. He put his grey hoodie on Charlotte and insisted we sit in his truck. Though I objected because of all the blood we had on us, his persistence won. I knew Charlotte needed to not look at the tragic scene, and LeeAnn needed to warm up.

The police and ambulance arrived rather quickly. Questions were asked, and statements were given. Not long after that, we loaded the two ambulances. Wes and Laura in one, and Charlotte, LeeAnn, me, and two officers boarded the second. The girls were checked again for injuries by the EMT. When we arrived at the hospital, our ambulance was locked while the first ambulance unloaded. So Charlotte would not hear, the officers quietly explained to me that if I cooperated, they would not have to handcuff me.

It was at that moment, the probability of the death of Wes and Laura and my guilt laid heavily upon me. I reassured the highway patrolmen they would have my full cooperation. The girls were taken away. Drug and alcohol tests were given to me. When the results came back clear, the girls were returned, and I was released from police custody.

Hard decisions followed, which all began with someone in a white coat holding a clipboard, paper, and pen. Laura did not look well, and despite all the efforts of the doctors and nurses, she grew worse not better. Though heart-wrenching, the first decision to make was obvious, signing to remove life support from Laura. We stood around her and watched her go. The next clipboard contained permission pages to donate Wes' organs and tissues if he were to pass away.

On our first date, Wes pulled out his wallet and showed me the place where he signed to be an organ donor, so most of those pages were easy. Then the hardest clipboard day of all came four days after the wreck when it was time to unplug the life-support equipment on my husband. We stood as a family and watched my strong husband fade.

My family was great. They helped through the whole process and supported me in every decision. We all drove back to my hometown together. There was a funeral, and more details and decisions were finalized. The biggest decision at that point was where the girls and I would live and what would I do. Though it was difficult to leave the support of my family in New Mexico, I knew I had to go back to Alexandria, Louisiana, to the church we were attending there. I knew my answer was in God.

It's hard to put into words how completely and utterly devastated I was. I was a young woman who relied heavily on my husband, and I was a bit of a controller. Okay, I really controlled everything. My husband couldn't leave my sight without my permission. I hated when he had

It's hard to put into words how completely and utterly devastated I was.

to be gone from my side. I needed him so badly, and I relied on him in every way.

It was devastating that night on the interstate to see him in the condition he was in—so mutilated. The strong man that I leaned on didn't look the same, and the condition of my little Laura was devastating. Everything was so horribly devastating.

How hard it was to walk away and know what to do. I was a baby Christian. We went to church, but I really didn't know a lot. So, I went back to my church. I knew to do that. I knew I needed God. I grew up Catholic—not that being Catholic is bad. I love the Catholic church. My family is Catholic, and I love them. There's a lot of people full of faith and God in the Catholic Church, but for me that was not what I needed. I knew I needed the Full Gospel Church we had started attending, and I knew I needed the Word of God.

I went back there with the girls. I was praying, and I was serious about hearing from God. You really can hear from God and know that you know that you know what He says. I knew whatever He said was what I was going to do.

I cried so much I had to put Q-tips in my ears to keep them from getting plugged up with water.

I prayed and asked God, "What do I do now?" He spoke to me often during that time. It's not spooky because God promises in

His Word that He's close to the brokenhearted. He spoke to me very clearly and said, "I want you to get up in the morning. I want you to praise Me. I want you to pray—pray for others and pray in the Spirit. And read the Word."

So, I did. I got up in the morning, and I started to worship God. It was really a revelation. It was a new thing to worship God in my own house. I thought the reason for worship in church was so people who were running late had a chance to get there. I didn't know there was any purpose other than that. In church we would sing songs and lift our hands to worship God because He is worthy. But I didn't realize anyone worshipped God in their own house. *How awkward*, I thought. But I did it. I started singing and worshipping God in my home just like God had told me.

During that time, I was absolutely amazed I actually had the fortitude to put one foot in front of the other. I felt like an empty shell. I would get up in the morning and do what God put in my heart for that day. When God gives you a word, He gives you a knowing or practical how-tos to get done what He's instructed you to do. He just kind of deposits them in your spirit. So, I would get up in the morning ready to do what He said.

It was hard to get up at 4:45 a.m. when you spent until 2 a.m. crying and feeling sorry for yourself. I called that time period "Years with Tears in My Ears." When you cry a lot standing up or sitting up, tears roll down your face. But if you cry a lot lying down, the tears all roll to your ears. I cried so much I had to put Q-tips in my ears to keep them from getting plugged up with water. Every night I would cry and feel sorry for myself until I fell asleep. But then I'd get up in the morning and start worshipping God. The more I grew in God, the less I felt sorry for myself.

At one point, I remembered a preacher who said something that really helped me. She said, "Never feel sorry for yourself. Never!" She experienced almost the same thing as I had, and she said, "Self-pity is nothing more than putting yourself in a pit." She had learned that she couldn't do anything if she was feeling sorry for herself. And that's the truth—you cannot. When you're feeling sorry for yourself, you're welcoming the devil to pile it on.

Eventually, I did stop feeling sorry for myself, but it's hard to do. In fact, you must make a firm decision not to feel sorry for yourself. As I got up in the morning and start worshipping God, I was tired. I was mad. I was sad. I was devastated. I wondered why. And my mind was filled with questions and thoughts like: *Why did this happen? How could this happen? We were tithers. We were givers. We worked in the children's church. We loved each other. Why? Why? Why?*

I would be so mad at God. Then I knew I shouldn't be mad at God, so I would apologize. All this was going on while I was singing. I was really just singing through my teeth. I would sing, "I worship You, Almighty God" with gritted teeth. "There is none like You" with gritted teeth. "Thank God for Your mercy" with gritted teeth. I was being obedient just not so willing. I was a brand-new Christian.

Wes and I had been going to church for about a year at that time, and the things I learned at church helped me. Just going to church helped me. I knew that I knew that I knew that God was worthy to be praised. I knew He was worthy. I knew He was a good God, and the devil was bad. I knew that all good and perfect things came from the Father above.

Yet I would wonder why these terrible things happened to me, and it took me a while to get it. When you're going to church, you may not think you're really getting anything. You think, *I have problems. I have this. I have that. Why go to church? I need a counselor. I need this. I need that.* But God's Word is amazing. It helps you whether you know it's helping you or not.

Back then, when we were first married, it was hard for us to go to church. We were a young couple with young kids and getting ready to go to church wasn't easy. There were all kinds of fights just getting out the door. You had to find shoes for the kids, and about the time you found one pair, you would lose another pair. We were tempted to think, *Why even go?* But, thank God, we went anyway. Looking back, let me tell you, it's important to go to church. Just put the kids in the car and forget the shoes. If you're going to fight, fight. Just get there!

During my recovery, I would get up in the morning and worship God while all these thoughts, feelings, and emotions were going through my head. I knew in my spirit that I just had to hang in there and stick with it. That's part of the knowing the Holy Ghost gives you to help you. I knew to just stay with it. I knew that to sing a couple of songs or read a couple of verses and walk away was not enough. I knew to stay with Him. So, I just kept singing and kept singing.

Day after day this continued. Eventually, I would get to the place where I would stop the whole gamut of, *Why? Why? Why?* with all the emotions and feelings of devastation. I would think, *I know this situation is awful. I know it hurts. It hurts so much I can't foresee ever feeling good again—ever. But even though my whole life is a mess and parts are missing, God is worthy to be praised. God is so worthy to be praised.* At that point, I would worship God with my whole being— my spirit, my mouth, my mind. I would say, "I worship You, Almighty God. There is none like You." If you're born again, your spirit is always ready to worship God.

As time passed, God healed me completely, but it's just so precious when I share my testimony. I relive that depth of that place where I was nothing. I had no joy—zero joy. But God would flood me with His presence as I would worship him with my heart, my mouth, and my mind. God would flood me with His joy. He would flood me with His peace. God would flood me with His life.

> God began to do a miracle in me, and I didn't feel like an empty shell anymore.

As I continued day after day and refused to

quit and give up, God began to do a miracle in me, and I didn't feel like an empty shell anymore. I would get full of the Holy Ghost and ready to go. I would read the Word, and every day it was so good. It was just for me. I loved it. I would write down scriptures and thoughts on a 3x5 card and keep it throughout the day. It would really help me because it's hard not to feel sorry for yourself. The devil doesn't play fair. He doesn't say, "Oh, you look like you're really suffering right now. You've gone through a lot. I'll come back later."

The devil is just the opposite of Jesus. Jesus says, "He will not crush the weakest reed or put out a flickering candle..." (Matthew 12:20 NLT). God's there to fan your flame and to heal the reed. God's there to strengthen, but the devil is there to cause as much hurt, harm, and agony as possible. The devil was there every second of my day to bombard me with thoughts of guilt: *It was your fault! It was your fault! It was your fault!* I could never get away from that. I hated myself so much. I knew it was my fault. I had a ten-page report from the Texas Rangers showing me how guilty I was. Yes, it was my fault, and I couldn't even look at myself in the mirror I hated myself so badly.

I had to overcome not only the sadness and the guilt but "the why." One day God helped me and said, "Carol, you just need to put *why* on the shelf." Every time I asked God why, it was worse than the last. Eventually, I had to put why on the shelf. And you can too.

I didn't use antidepressants to get over the great loss, pain, and guilt. God healed me! That's not to say antidepressants

God helped me with the guilt, the sorrow, and the sadness.

are completely wrong, but God can help you. The medicines can ease symptoms, but only God can heal your broken heart.

God helped me with the guilt, the sorrow, and the sadness. I was a new Christian, and I didn't know all these things. I didn't know there was a "sacrifice of praise" until God led me to praise. I worshipped God with all my heart, my mind, and my mouth whether I was mowing the lawn, cooking dinner, paying bills, or whatever.

I worshipped God.

And I had to do something else to get over the guilt that haunted me. I had to take the Word of God and extinguish every thought.

2 Corinthians 10:4-5

For the weapons of our warfare are not carnal but mighty in God for pulling down strongholds, casting down arguments and every high thing that exalts itself against the knowledge of God, bringing every thought into captivity to the obedience of Christ.

I had to find something in the Bible to help me because I was guilty. The wreck was my fault. But, praise God, I found the help I needed in God's Word.

Isaiah 53:4-5 (AMPC)

*Surely He has borne our griefs (sicknesses, weaknesses, and distresses) and carried our sorrows and pains [of punishment], yet we [ignorantly] considered Him stricken, smitten, and afflicted by God [as if with leprosy]. **But He was wounded for our transgressions, He was bruised for our guilt and** iniquities; the chastisement [needful to obtain] peace and well-being for us was upon Him, and with the stripes [that wounded] Him we are healed and made whole.*

I saw it right there in the Word. "He [Jesus] was wounded for our transgressions and He bore our **guilt and iniquities.**" Jesus carried our guilt. He bore my guilt!

Colossians 1:22 says:

*In the body of His flesh through death, **to present you holy, and blameless, and above reproach in His sight....***

Colossians says that He's made us holy and **blameless** and above reproach. He made me holy, blameless, praise God!

Ephesians 1:4 says almost the same thing:

> *Just as He chose us in Him before the foundation of the world, that we should be holy and **without blame** before Him in love.*

These scriptures were my ammunition, and there were whole entire days and weeks I spent fighting my thoughts. I had to make sure to think the Word because if I thought three other thoughts in a row, I was overcome with guilt. I would sink to places where I was so deeply depressed, I would lock myself in a dark room with a knife at my throat.

These scriptures were my ammunition, and there were whole entire days and weeks I spent fighting my thoughts.

I won't go into too many details on that topic because it isn't edifying to hear, but clearly, I just didn't want to live. Now, listen to me! You don't have to think those thoughts. You don't have to think every thought that comes into your mind.

What's so amazing about those really dark days when I was in the closet, is most of the time they were Saturdays. I called them "the Saturday devils" that tormented me. I would end up in the closet almost every Saturday. The thing is, our church had prayer on Saturday night. All day I would feel sorry for myself in that dark closet, but at five o'clock Saturday I knew I had to go to prayer. And I did. Everything would be better after that.

You *can* choose your thoughts. You **can** help what you think!

Think about the demoniac of Gadara. He had an entire legion of devils harassing him. But when he chose to go to Jesus, not one of the devils—or all of them together—could stop him.

You can choose what you think just as I could choose what I would think. I chose the Word of God. The Word was far greater than my circumstance. I thought on the Word, and it healed me. It made me completely whole.

When you break your arm or leg, you go to the hospital. They bind you up and send you home. But when you go to God with a broken heart, the Doctor goes home with you. I fell in love with the Doctor. I fell in love with Jesus. I fell in love with God. He's so very good.

I've heard about a lot of women and men who go through tragedy and struggle as I did. They ask, "Why did this happen?" or "Why did this person do this or that to me?" I've heard divorced people say, "Look what my former spouse has done and is doing to me." These people are angry, hurt, and bitter. But being angry, hurt, and bitter doesn't change anything.

What do you do?

You go to God!

No matter what feelings are crushing you or what thoughts are bombarding your mind, you can go to God. Then you can grow up in Him by feeding on His Word. The more we get in God, the more we have a fighting spirit and a spirit of joy. God is so good, and He will make you completely whole.

I remember feeling like I lived with a constant pain in the pit of my stomach for a little more than two years. There's no automatic one-year, two-year, three-year, four-year timing to overcome regrets or depression or a broken heart. But if you stay with it, complete healing and total deliverance will surely come. God gives you His Word on it!

For me, it was about two and a half years after the tragedy that there was no more pain. It was gone. I got to enjoy God and enjoy life again.

There are two more scriptures I want to share with you that really helped me:

Deuteronomy 29:29

The secret things belong to the Lord our God,
but those things which are revealed belong to
us and to our children forever, that we may
do all the words of this law.

This scripture helped me put "the why" on the shelf. Like it or not, why and how some things happen is God's business—not ours.

Here's another scripture that helped me on those many Saturdays I spent in the closet:

Psalm 27:13

I would have lost heart, unless I had believed that I would see the goodness of the LORD IN THE LAND OF THE LIVING.

This scripture helped me because it promised me that I would see the goodness of the Lord in the land of the living. In other words, things would get better here on earth, not just get better in heaven someday.

If you're suffering like I was, you can ask Jesus right now to heal your broken heart and set you free—free from sadness, depression, loneliness, addiction, and regrets of the past. Ask Him to show you the supernatural power of God.

Jesus will put your broken heart back together again. He will put your life together. He will give you joy, love, and vision. He will make you fruitful and empower you to make a positive impact on your world. The gospel will do things in your life that will make a difference—not just for you but for everyone

> No matter what feelings are crushing you or what thoughts are bombarding your mind, you can go to God.

around you. That was the invitation God gave in Psalms when He said, "Taste and see that the Lord is good."

Jesus is saying to you, "Just give Me a chance!"

Some people will go to every doctor in town. They will try every expert opinion they can find, but I dare you to give Jesus a chance. Let Jesus work on your problem. He'll set you free from your past just like He set me free from mine.

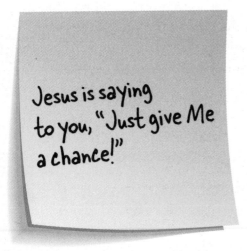

Jesus is saying to you, "Just give Me a chance!"

CHAPTER 13

LIVING WITH NO
Regrets Scriptures

The Word of God works! As you speak it, meditate on it, and get it down on the inside of you, it will replace feelings of sorrow, sadness, and regret and displace the pain associated with them. This doesn't happen instantly, but over time as you speak and meditate on these powerful promises from God's Word, change *will* come.

Proverbs 4:22 says of God's words, "For they are life unto those that find them, and health to all their flesh." The word *health* in Hebrew means *medicine*. God's Word works like medicine. It works over time. If your doctor prescribed six weeks of medication for a certain ailment, you wouldn't get discouraged or give up if the symptoms weren't gone after one dose. You would give it time to work. So, give the Word time to do its work in your life. Speak these words over your life daily, and depending on your need, go over them two or three or more times a day. You cannot overdose on God's Word!

The following verses were the basis for the teaching in this book. They are listed here for your convenience and divided into different sections. Get familiar with the scriptures that deal with your area of concern by memorizing them, reading them out loud, and meditating on them. If you will take the time to confess these scriptures and read the confessions at the end of each section, it will change your life!

> Over time as you speak and meditate on these powerful promises from God's Word, change will come.

GET READY FOR YOUR FUTURE
by Getting Over Your Past!

No matter how much you've done wrong or how little you've done right, Jesus can set you free from regret. *Regret* is a feeling of sorrow or remorse for a fault, act, loss, disappointment, etc. But you *can* overcome it!

Revelation 21:4

And God will wipe away every tear from their eyes; there shall be no more death, nor sorrow, nor crying. There shall be no more pain, for the former things have passed away.

Isaiah 53:4-5 (AMPC)

Surely He has borne our griefs (sicknesses, weaknesses, and distresses) and carried our sorrows and pains [of punishment], yet we [ignorantly] considered Him stricken, smitten, and afflicted by God [as if with leprosy]. But He was wounded for our transgressions, He was bruised for our guilt and iniquities; the chastisement [needful to obtain] peace and well-being for us was upon Him, and with the stripes [that wounded] Him we are healed and made whole.

Luke 2:10

*Then the angel said to them, "Do not be afraid, for behold, I bring you **good tidings** of **great joy** which will be to all people."*

1 Peter 1:8 (NLT)

*whom having not seen you love. Though now you do not see Him, yet believing, you **rejoice with joy inexpressible and full of glory,** and you **rejoice with a glorious, inexpressible joy.***

Confession: No one has a perfect past, but I now choose to apply what Jesus did to my past. Jesus has paid the price for God to wipe away every tear. I accept what He did. He bore my griefs and carried my sorrows. Jesus' coming brought good tidings of great joy to me. I believe in what Jesus did, and therefore, I rejoice with a glorious, inexpressible joy!

MISSED OPPORTUNITIES, Disappointment, and Regret

Joel 2:25

So I will restore to you the years that the swarming locust has eaten, the crawling locust, the consuming locust, and the chewing locust....

Psalm 103:13-14

As a father pities his children, So the Lord pities those who fear Him. For He knows our frame; He remembers that we are dust.

Psalm 103:13-14 (NLT)

The Lord is like a father to his children, tender and compassionate to those who fear him. For he knows how weak we are; he remembers we are only dust.

Psalm 147:3

He heals the brokenhearted and binds up their wounds.

Confession: My Father restores the years that bad choices have robbed from me, and He removes all regret and sadness associated with them. My Father is tender and compassionate toward me, and He knows my limitations.

PAST SINS, GUILT, AND SHAME

Isaiah 53:5

*But He was wounded for our transgressions, He was bruised for our iniquities; the **chastisement** for our **peace** was upon Him, And by His stripes we are healed.*

Matthew 1:21

And she will bring forth a Son, and you shall call His name Jesus, for He will save His people from their sins.

Hebrews 9:12

Not with the blood of goats and calves, but with His own blood He entered the Most Holy Place once for all, having obtained eternal redemption.

Hebrews 9:14

How much more shall the blood of Christ, who through the eternal Spirit offered Himself without spot to God, cleanse your conscience from dead works to serve the living God?

Hebrews 10:12

But this Man, after He had offered one sacrifice for sins forever, sat down at the right hand of God.

Hebrews 10:17-18

Then He adds, "Their sins and their lawless deeds I will remember no more." Now where there is remission of these, there is no longer an offering for sin.

Hebrews 10:22

Let us draw near with a true heart in full assurance of faith, having our hearts sprinkled from an evil conscience and our bodies washed with pure water.

Colossians 2:14 (KJV)

Blotting out the handwriting of ordinances that was against us, which was contrary to us, and took it out of the way, nailing it to his cross....

Romans 8:33-34 (KJV)

Who shall lay any thing to the charge of God's elect? It is God that justifieth. Who is he that condemneth? It is Christ that died, yea rather, that is risen again, who is even at the right hand of God, who also maketh intercession for us.

Daniel 11:35

And some of those of understanding shall fall, to refine them, purify them, and make them white, until the time of the end; because it is still for the appointed time.

1 John 3:21

Beloved, if our heart does not condemn us, we have confidence toward God.

Confession: Jesus was wounded for my transgressions and bruised for my iniquities. He has forgiven me of all my sins. Since I am forgiven, I no longer accept the symptoms of guilt, condemnation, and shame. My heart no longer condemns me, and I have confidence toward God.

BROKEN RELATIONSHIPS, Sadness, and Sorrow

Romans 12:18

If it is possible, as much as depends on you, live peaceably with all men.

Mark 11:25

And whenever you stand praying, if you have anything against anyone, forgive him, that your Father in heaven may also forgive you your trespasses.

Isaiah 53:4

*Surely He has **borne** our **griefs** and **carried** our **sorrows**....*

Psalm 147:3

He heals the brokenhearted and binds up their wounds.

1 Peter 3:9

Not returning evil for evil or reviling for reviling, but on the contrary blessing, knowing that you were called to this, that you may inherit a blessing.

Confession: I've done my best to do right by everyone. I've asked for forgiveness where I was wrong, and I forgive anyone who has done anything to me. Therefore, I no longer allow grief and sorrow to haunt me over broken relationships. I bless everyone, and I refuse to curse them. I know that any relationship I fail to restore on earth, Jesus will restore in heaven.

LOSS OF A LOVED ONE, Grief, and Mourning

Isaiah 61:3

To console those who mourn in Zion, to give them beauty for ashes, the oil of joy for mourning, the garment of praise for the spirit of heaviness; that they may be called trees of righteousness, the planting of the Lord, that He may be glorified.

Deuteronomy 29:29

The secret things belong to the Lord our God, but those things which are revealed belong to us and to our children forever, that we may do all the words of this law.

Jeremiah 30:17

"For I will restore health to you and heal you of your wounds," says the Lord....

Luke 4:18

The Spirit of the Lord is upon Me, because He has anointed Me to preach the gospel to the poor; He has sent Me to heal the broken-hearted, to proclaim liberty to the captives and recovery of sight to the blind, to set at liberty those who are oppressed.

Psalm 147:3

He heals the brokenhearted and binds up their wounds.

Psalm 30:10-12

"Hear, O Lord, and have mercy on me; Lord, be my helper!" You have turned for me my mourning into dancing; You have put off my sackcloth and clothed me with gladness, to the end that my glory may sing praise to You and not be silent. O Lord my God, I will give thanks to You forever.

Confession: Thank you, Jesus, for healing my broken heart. You turned my mourning into dancing and clothed me with gladness. I release my loved one to the glories of heaven and honor their life by celebrating our reunion.

FREE TO BE HAPPY

Revelation 12:11

And they overcame him by the blood of the Lamb and by the word of their testimony, and they did not love their lives to the death.

Romans 8:11

But if the Spirit of Him who raised Jesus from the dead dwells in you, He who raised Christ from the dead will also give life to your mortal bodies through His Spirit who dwells in you.

1 John 4:4

You are of God, little children, and have overcome them, because He who is in you is greater than he who is in the world.

Ephesians 1:3-7

*Blessed be the God and Father of our Lord Jesus Christ, who has **blessed** us with every spiritual blessing in the heavenly places in Christ, just as He **chose** us in Him before the foundation of the world, that we should be holy and **without blame** before Him in love, having predestined us to **adoption** as sons by Jesus Christ to Himself, according to the good pleasure of His will, to the praise of the glory of His grace, by which He made us **accepted** in the Beloved. In Him we have **redemption** through His blood, the **forgiveness** of sins, according to the riches of His grace.*

2 Corinthians 5:21

For He made Him who knew no sin to be sin for us, that we might become the righteousness of God in Him.

Psalm 126:1-3

*When the Lord brought back the captivity of Zion, we were like those who dream. Then our mouth was filled with laughter, And our tongue with singing. Then they said among the nations, "The Lord has done great things for them." The Lord has done great things for us, and **we are glad.***

Psalm 144:15

Happy are the people who are in such a state; Happy are the people whose God is the Lord!

Confession: I overcome by the blood of the Lamb and the word of my testimony. The same Spirit that raised Christ from the dead dwells in me, and greater is He who lives in me than he who is in the world. According to the New Testament, I am blessed, chosen, blameless, adopted, accepted, redeemed, forgiven, and righteous. Because the Lord has done great things for me, my mouth is filled with laughter, and I am glad. No more sadness! No more sorrow! No more regrets!

A GIFT
For You

If you are looking for a change in your life or if you are seeking a peace that is found through a personal relationship with a loving God, then He is ready and willing to help you—right now and right where you are.

Salvation is a gift that is made available to those who repent, believe, and confess that Jesus is Lord. Jesus died and rose from the dead to save mankind (Acts 16:31; Romans 10:9-10). This gift cannot be received through good deeds or by simply being a good person (Ephesians 2:8, 1 Timothy 1:9). It's received by faith—by believing and acting on God's Word concerning salvation.

Pray this prayer aloud, now:

Heavenly Father, I come to You in the name of Jesus. Your Word says, "whoever calls on the name of the Lord shall be saved" (Acts 2:21). I am calling on You.

I pray and ask Jesus to come into my heart and be Lord and Savior over my life. According to Romans 10:9-10, "If you confess with your mouth the Lord Jesus and believe in your heart that God has raised Him from the dead, you will be saved."

I do that now. I confess Jesus as my Lord, and I believe in my heart that God raised Him from the dead.

If you have prayed this prayer, welcome to the family of God! Share your good news with us and let us know what God has done in your life.

GREG FRITZ MINISTRIES

For more information about Greg Fritz Ministries
or a listing of additional teaching materials, visit
www. gregfritz.org
or write to us at
P.O. Box 700900, Tulsa, OK 74170.

ABOUT THE AUTHOR

Greg Fritz has been traveling around the world since 1989, teaching and preaching God's Word throughout the United States and overseas. His travels have included ministry in more than 25 nations. Emphasizing the topics of faith and redemption, Greg regularly ministers with signs following in churches, Bible schools, seminars and many other outreaches. A graduate of RHEMA Bible Training Center, Greg and his wife, Carol, make their home in Tulsa, Oklahoma.

ANOTHER BOOK BY GREG FRITZ

It seems bad news is covering the globe these days. A steady diet of negative reports is unhealthy, depressing, and paralyzing. Yet, God has GOOD NEWS for you! It's news so good the bad news won't matter anymore.

Author and minister Greg Fritz shares GOOD NEWS from God's Word that will uplift, liberate and empower you. These truths will help you see where you came from, why you're here, who you are, and where you're going.

This book is simple enough for a new believer yet includes a systematic study of man's redemption deep enough to enrich any student of the Bible. It's written in a way that takes ancient Bible doctrines and applies them to the problems and challenges we all face today.

The Harrison House Vision

Proclaiming the truth and the power
of the Gospel of Jesus Christ with excellence.
Challenging Christians
to live victoriously,
grow spiritually,
know God intimately.

Connect with us on
 Facebook @ HarrisonHousePublishers
and Instagram @ HarrisonHousePublishing
so you can stay up to date with news
about our books and our authors.

Visit us at **www.harrisonhouse.com**
for a complete product listing as well as
monthly specials for wholesale distribution.